HOW DOES THAT MAKE YOU FEEL?

HOW DOES THAT MAKE YOU FEEL?

WHY MODERN THERAPY'S COMFORT-FIRST APPROACH FAILS TO BRING TRUE CHANGE

Dr Chuck Carrington

CONNECT BOOKS

This is a work of nonfiction. Some parts have been fictionalized in varying degrees, for various purposes.

Copyright © 2025 CP Carrington
all rights reserved

ISBN 979-8-9892386-8-2 (paperback edition)

Printed by Connect Books in the United States of America

Connect Books

USA

PO BOX 903 Wakefield VA. USA 23888
Connectbooks.pub

All rights reserved. No part of this book may be reproduced in any form or by an electronic or mechanical means, including information storage and retrieval systems, without permission in writing from the publisher, except by a reviewer who may quote brief passages in a review

Unless otherwise noted, all Scripture quotations are taken from the Holy Bible, New International Version® (NIV). Copyright © by Biblica, Inc. Used by Permission.

Dedication

To my mentor, Dr. Merrill Reese the *"Great One"* —who, among the many lessons he gave me, taught first and foremost the power of listening. Not merely to hear words, but to be fully *present*—to attend to what was truly being said. To grasp meaning beneath language, to sense the feelings behind the silence, and to follow the subtle clues and quiet hunches that would guide clients toward healing. Whatever success I have known with clients began with him.

Contents

Author's Personal Note: 1
Prologue: The Sacred Gift of Presence 3
Chapter 1 Can Counseling Become an Addiction? 9
Chapter 2: The Rise of Feelings-First Therapy 21
Chapter 3: The Impact of Multicultural Eclecticism and Moral Relativism 41
Chapter 4: The Advocacy Problem in Professional Counseling 53
Chapter 5: Emotional Reasoning and the Death of Objective Truth 65
Chapter 6: Gentle Parenting, Weak Men, and Me-First Relationships 77
Chapter 7: SEL in Schools—A Systematic Reinforcement of Narcissism 89
Chapter 8: The Over-Emphasis on Feelings 101
Chapter 9: The Missing Link—Lack of Intellectual Challenge 111
Chapter 10: The Fear of Guidance and Action 121
Chapter 11: A Framework for Healthy Counseling 133
Chapter 12: Correcting the Course—What Parents, Educators, and Churches Can Do 143
Chapter 13: A Call to Reform Counseling 153
Chapter 14: The Way Back 163

Author's Personal Note:

Before we begin, let me be clear: this is ***not*** an anti-therapy book. I believe deeply in the power of counseling. I've devoted my life to the work of helping people heal. But I also believe we must be honest about the drift we've seen in the profession. Not all therapy is good therapy. Not all counselors are equipped to guide. And not every framework that affirms the client's point of view, beliefs, or position is actually helping.

This book is written from within the field—not as an outsider throwing stones, but as a practitioner sounding the alarm. I want to see counseling return to its roots: courageous presence, moral clarity, and transformative growth. If we don't challenge the current direction, we risk losing what made this profession sacred in the first place.

Prologue: The Sacred Gift of Presence

There's something sacred that happens when you sit with someone—not just in the same room, but truly *with* them. Eye to eye. Shoulder to shoulder. Heart to heart. In the quiet moments when words slow and the soul speaks, something deeper than conversation begins to unfold. You feel it when a grieving friend finally exhales the weight they've carried for months, or when a spouse sits in the rawness of truth and is met not with judgment, but with understanding. That sacred something is presence. And I believe it is one of the most powerful gifts we can offer another human being.

When I think about what it means to be present as a counselor, I cannot help but be drawn into the deeper, richer story of how God was first present with us. Long before the therapeutic world gave us the language of empathy, attunement, and relational neuroscience, there was Jesus—the Son of God who stepped into the dust of our world to walk among us. This wasn't symbolic or theoretical. It was literal. God left heaven and moved into our neighborhood. And in doing so, He gave us the ultimate model of what it means to be present.

John writes in his Gospel, "The Word became flesh and made His dwelling among us" (John 1:14). Those words aren't just theological. They're relational. God didn't send a messenger or broadcast a distant signal from the sky. He came Himself. He looked into our eyes. He felt the limitations of a human body. He wept real tears. He laughed with friends. He grieved in gardens. He entered the phenomenon of human experience so that we could know Him—not just in concept, but in relationship.

This is the heart of the sacred gift of presence. That God would choose to be *with* us. And that His presence would become the doorway to healing, redemption, and restored relationship.

I remember a young woman named Kayla who came to counseling barely able to speak. Her trauma was buried deep beneath years of silence, shame, and a stoic kind of survival. In our early sessions, she'd sit with her hands clenched in her lap, eyes down, words clipped and cautious. I didn't push. I didn't press. I simply stayed. Week after week, I met her in that quiet space. Slowly, her fists loosened. Her voice found its way back. And one day, she looked at me through tears and whispered, "I didn't think anyone could sit with my pain without trying to fix it." That's the sacred gift of presence. It isn't about fixing. It's about being.

Jesus didn't come to earth to fix us like a technician might repair a broken appliance. He came to be with us, to suffer with us, to walk with us. In doing so, He gave us a new way to understand healing—not as a task to accomplish, but as a relationship to enter.

As counselors, we enter into the phenomenology of our clients—their lived experiences, their memories, their hopes, and their fears. We don't merely analyze or interpret. We enter. We attune. We become students of their inner world, not to conquer it or control it, but to honor it. This is the Christlike path of presence.

Think about the woman at the well in John 4. Jesus didn't ignore her pain or lecture her about her lifestyle. He met her in the heat of the day, at a place of isolation, and He listened. He engaged her story. He revealed truth not through accusation, but through presence. His nearness broke down her defenses. His attentiveness gave her dignity. His truth-telling came not as condemnation, but as invitation.

That same dynamic unfolds in the sacred space of a counseling room. When we are present with someone—not just physically, but emotionally and spiritually present—we create a space where defenses can lower and the soul can rise. It's not about technique. It's about posture. Presence isn't a skill we perform; it's a person we become.

I recall a young father named Marcus who came into therapy after a bitter divorce. He was angry, sharp-edged, and bracing for a fight. The first session, he sat with arms crossed, eyes darting, looking for any reason to distrust me. But something shifted when I simply said, "This seems like it's been a long road, and I imagine you're tired." He looked up. Just a flicker. And that was the beginning. I didn't argue. I didn't interpret. I just stayed. And over time, Marcus stopped bracing and started sharing. Presence did what logic could not. It opened the door.

God's presence does the same. It doesn't bulldoze our walls. It waits at the door and knocks. And when we open even slightly, He comes in. Not to shame us, but to sit with us. Not to scold, but to shepherd. This is the relational ministry of Jesus—incarnational, patient, attuned.

Christian counseling, at its best, mirrors that same ministry. We are not just professionals offering insight. We are companions offering presence. And that presence becomes sacred when it is offered with the humility and attentiveness of Christ.

There is something holy about entering into someone else's story. Their sorrows and joys. Their regrets and dreams. To sit with someone in their brokenness without rushing them toward a solution is to say, "You matter. Right here. As you are." And isn't that the message of the Gospel? That while we were still sinners, Christ died for us? Not after we had cleaned ourselves up or worked through our issues, but in the very midst of our mess.

Presence honors the process. It doesn't rush the story. It doesn't demand a tidy ending. It stays, even when the narrative is jagged and unresolved. That's what Jesus did. He stayed. Through misunderstanding, betrayal, abandonment—even unto death. And in His staying, He healed.

There's a passage in Isaiah that has always moved me: "In all their distress, He too was distressed, and the angel of His presence saved them" (Isaiah 63:9). The angel of His presence. What a phrase. It tells us that God doesn't stand above our suffering; He enters it. His nearness becomes our rescue.

As counselors, we don't have wings. We don't walk on water. But we do carry the image of the One who did. And when we sit with a client in love, without agenda, with deep empathy and compassionate regard, we become vessels of that same angelic presence. Not to save, but to serve. Not to fix, but to accompany.

Presence is costly. It means setting aside our own need to be impressive or efficient. It means resisting the urge to give quick answers or solve someone else's pain. It requires patience, humility, and trust—trust that God is doing more in the quiet space of relationship than we could accomplish with a thousand clever interventions.

I've often said that counseling is less about what we say and more about who we are. The therapeutic relationship is the crucible where healing is forged. Not because we have power, but because we reflect the presence of the One who does.

So, to every Christian counselor reading this, I want to say: your presence matters. You are doing more than listening. You are ministering. When you show up fully, when you listen deeply, when you stay faithfully—you are echoing the heart of Christ. You are becoming the hands and heart of God to someone who may not know that He is still near.

And to every person who has experienced the pain of being unseen, unheard, or misunderstood—I want you to know: God is not distant. He is not passive. He came to be with you. And He still is. In the quiet. In the sorrow. In the questions and in the waiting. He is present. He is Emmanuel, God with us.

May this book, and this journey we are about to take together, begin not with answers, but with presence. May we learn to be with one another as God has been with us. And in that sacred space, may we find the healing that only His presence can bring.

Welcome to the sacred gift of presence.

Chapter 1
Can Counseling Become an Addiction?
An Obsession With Feelings

As a counselor and educator, I've spent decades walking alongside people in emotional pain. I've also spent years training counselors to do the same. But over time, I've begun to ask a difficult question—not from cynicism, but from concern: *Can counseling itself contribute to emotional addiction?*

We know that emotions can produce powerful biochemical effects in the brain. Intense emotional experiences trigger the release of endorphins and dopamine—neurochemicals associated with reward and pleasure. When dopamine is released, it creates a sense of satisfaction, even euphoria, which in turn reinforces the behavior that produced it.

This is the foundation of what we call **process addictions**—behaviors that create internal reward cycles without the introduction of a foreign substance. Unlike substance addiction, where the high comes from alcohol or drugs, process addiction relies on the body's own chemistry. The behavior becomes its own drug. Whether it's gambling, shopping, or pornography, the brain begins to chase the dopamine hit that these behaviors produce.

But what if emotions—specifically *emotional expression*—can function in the same way?

Some researchers and clinicians have long postulated the idea of *feelings addiction*. In my own clinical work, I've encountered clients who appear to have developed an unhealthy dependency on certain emotional states—particularly *anger, outrage*, or a sense of moral superiority. These clients often fit the profile of what some refer to as "injustice collectors." They spend an inordinate amount of time cataloging offenses, real or perceived, and seeking opportunities to assert their grievances.

They may not be chasing resolution, healing, or peace. Instead, they seem to be chasing the **feeling** itself—the emotional intensity that comes from righteous indignation, blame, or even vengeance. We see cultural caricatures of this in the so-called "Karen" archetype—individuals who insert themselves into others' affairs with disproportionate intensity, often under the guise of enforcing justice or correcting wrongs. These behaviors are rarely rational, and even when met with resistance or social disapproval, the behavior persists.

That persistence tells us something: they're being rewarded. But not with social affirmation, justice, financial gain, or relational closeness. In fact, their behavior often results in isolation or public backlash. So where's the payoff?

It seems clear that the reward is *internal*—a dopamine surge linked to the emotional charge itself. As Dr. Anna Lembke[1] describes in her book *Dopamine Nation*, we are living in a time where dopamine-driven behaviors are increasingly normalized and even encouraged. If we can become addicted to anything that produces dopamine, then yes—we can become addicted to **feelings**.

And here's where my concern turns inward—toward my own profession.

As counselors, we have built a field around *emotional exploration*. Rightfully so. Many people have been denied the language, space, or safety to feel and process emotions. Therapy, at its best, creates that space. But somewhere along the way, we may have *over corrected*. In our efforts to validate feelings, we've allowed the process to stall in *emotional expression* without helping clients move forward into insight and change.

The result? Clients may become overly attached to the emotional stage of the therapeutic process—revisiting their pain, reactivating emotional responses, and becoming dependent on the experience of *being heard* as the primary form of healing.

---

[1] Lembke, A. (2021). *Dopamine nation: finding balance in the age of indulgence*. Dutton.

But healing doesn't end with exploration. In fact, that's only the beginning.

Of course, emotional exploration by itself isn't always a dead end. For some clients—especially those with developmental trauma, emotional neglect, or suppressed grief—just naming the feeling is the first and most critical breakthrough. I once worked with a young man named Elias who had never been allowed to express sadness as a child. His emotional world had been limited to anger or silence. In our early work together, simply identifying sadness—not analyzing it or fixing it—brought visible relief. He cried, for the first time in years, and told me, "No one ever told me I was allowed to feel this." That moment of permission became the doorway to deeper insight. The problem isn't emotional validation—it's stopping there.

When clients stay in emotional expression without being challenged to examine their beliefs, confront their patterns, or take action, they are not being helped—they're being held back.

As counselors, we must reflect on this. Have we, in our compassion, inadvertently trained our clients to become emotionally dependent? Have we modeled a therapeutic process that soothes but doesn't stretch, that listens but doesn't lead?

This book will explore that question. Not to dismantle the value of emotional work, but to reframe it within a more complete model of growth—one that moves beyond feelings, into *insight*, and finally into *transformation*.

Real change doesn't happen just by feeling more. It happens by understanding, challenging, and acting on what we feel. And as counselors, we are called to guide that process—not just affirm it.

Let me explain…

The Overemphasis on Feelings: A Counselor's Reflection

As both a counselor and a counselor educator, I can tell you without hesitation: feelings matter. Emotions are not optional in therapy—they're foundational. But over the years, I've come to see that focusing on feelings, though necessary, is not enough.

When I was in graduate school—years ago, across multiple programs—we were required to do something I dreaded but dutifully completed: the verbatim transcript. We'd record our mock sessions with practice clients, and then painstakingly transcribe them, word for word. Once transcribed, we would analyze those sessions—deconstructing what we said, how we responded, and what the client was likely experiencing in the moment. We'd assess what we did well and what we might have done differently.

It was a powerful exercise—humbling, frustrating, and essential.

My earliest transcripts were recorded on VHS tapes (yes, I still have a few). What strikes me most now when I rewatch them? Sure, I had more hair back then, and none of it was gray. But more importantly, I see just how much I had to learn.

Our professors would watch the tapes and then return our written transcripts marked up with red ink. My professor would circle every feeling word expressed by the client and draw a line connecting it to my response—if I had acknowledged or reflected it. If I didn't, she'd mark it with a question or a reminder: *"Why didn't you connect to this feeling?"*

This was the first critique on nearly every transcript. The message was clear: *feelings come first.*

When I began teaching counseling skills years later, I found myself repeating the same advice: *"If you get stuck, go back to the feeling."* If you're unsure where the session is going, pull for the feeling. If you're uncertain about what the client needs, explore the feeling. Why? Because feelings are diagnostic. They give us a readout on what's going on inside the heart.

It's not unlike taking a car to the mechanic. The mechanic doesn't always hear the problem directly—he connects the car to a code reader. When a fault code comes up, he knows what system to investigate. In the same way, feelings are emotional fault codes. They point to where something deeper needs attention.

This is what we teach counselors to do—read the code. So it makes sense that counselor education focuses heavily on emotion. We spend countless hours training students to ask, *"What are you feeling?" "What does that feeling mean to you?" "Tell me more about that feeling."*

And again, this isn't wrong. In fact, it's essential. Feelings tell us where to look. They point us to the wound. But diagnosing the problem doesn't fix it.

That's where I began to notice something missing—not in theory, but in practice.

As a counselor, I don't send my clients to psychologists or psychiatrists just to get a diagnosis. I already know the diagnosis. A psychiatrist might say, *"You have depression"*— but that's not helpful if all we do is name it and medicate it. That's like noticing your car is making a terrible noise and deciding to just turn up the radio so you don't hear it anymore. That's what antidepressants often do—they turn the volume down, but they don't fix what's broken underneath.

Likewise, I don't refer clients to a diagnostician to "listen" unless we already know there's an organic issue that needs medication. Psychologists and psychiatrists are trained to identify, not necessarily to heal. That's what counselors do. We listen for the codes, yes—but then we go deeper. Or at least, we should.

Here's the heart of it: feelings are diagnostic, not reparative.

In the most basic sense, counseling involves three core stages. Models vary—some describe five stages, others seven or nine—but they all boil down to three essentials:[2]

> ***Exploration*** – identifying the emotion
>
> ***Insight*** – understanding the reason behind it
>
> ***Action*** – changing what needs to change

Counselor education does a great job teaching the first stage. We train our students to listen, reflect, validate, and explore emotion. We teach them to be emotionally attuned and relationally present. And that's a gift to the profession.

But too often, we stop there. We don't train them well to move clients into insight, and we rarely train them to coach clients into action.

Early in my training, one of my professors—himself a seasoned traumatologist and grief counselor—warned me: *"Be careful when pulling for too many feelings. If you don't help the client move into insight, you may flood them."* I've never forgotten that. He was the only professor, in fourteen years of education, to ever bother to warn me about the danger of emotional flooding. The rest emphasized emotional exploration without caution.

---

[2] Beck, J. S. (2011). *Cognitive Behavior Therapy: Basics and Beyond*. Guilford Press.

Neenan, M., & Dryden, W. (2004). *Cognitive Therapy: 100 Key Points and Techniques*. Routledge.

But he understood the deeper work. He was more than a teacher—he was a practitioner. And that makes a difference.

Yes, clients need to feel. They need space to name and understand what's going on inside. But then what? That's the missing piece in much of modern therapy.

Clients often rejoice when they identify a feeling. And rightly so—it brings a kind of emotional relief. They may even feel empowered by expressing it. And when the counselor affirms this moment, the client feels validated. But here's the catch: each of those steps triggers a dopamine reward.

> Feel—express—validate…Reward.
> Feel—express—validate…Reward.
> Rinse and repeat as often as possible.

This can become a cycle of emotional reward without forward motion. The client comes into the session emotionally distressed, they express their feelings, they feel relief, they're praised for their insight—and they leave feeling better. But if nothing has changed in their life, they'll be back the next week to do it again. And again. And again.

Could this be therapy addiction? Or feelings addiction?

I'm not entirely sure. But I do believe it's possible. And I think we need to start asking the question.

Because if we stop at emotion, we do our clients a disservice. To be an effective counselor, you must take the client from feeling to understanding to action.

Insight means asking, *"Why am I feeling this way?"* Not just in the moment, but at the core. What is lacking in my life that allows this emotion to dominate my reactions? What unresolved wound, what belief system, what relational pattern is giving this feeling such power?

Feelings are not facts. They are interpretations—momentary reflections of what we *believe* about something. And beliefs can change. Which means emotional states can change too—but not just by feeling them more deeply. They change when we begin to understand their root and do something about it.

When your car is running rough, you don't congratulate yourself for noticing. You fix it. When your child cries from an ear infection, you don't turn up the music—you treat the infection. And when someone is depressed, knowing *that* they're depressed doesn't solve the problem. You must uncover the *why*, and then act on that knowledge.

In graduate school, another professor gave me a simple but powerful framework as I prepared for my first major research presentation. I was overwhelmed with all the data I had collected, unsure of how to present it meaningfully. She said, *"Just remember: what, so what, and now what."*

What is the issue you're identifying?

So what is why it matters to the audience, to the field, and to the clients we serve.

Now what is the action you're calling for. What needs to change?

It hit me like a lightbulb. That was exactly what I had learned years earlier in my counseling skills class: exploration, insight, and action.

And that's what I'm inviting you to consider now.

We cannot afford to be counselors who only explore. We must be counselors who help our clients understand and then transform. The soul does not heal by validation alone. It heals when insight leads to growth—and growth leads to change.

That's what this book is about.

Chapter 2:
The Rise of Feelings-First Therapy

How Emotional Validation Replaced Personal Growth in Modern Counseling

In the early days of professional counseling, the therapeutic process was designed to guide individuals through a structured journey: first, to explore their emotional landscape; next, to gain cognitive insight into the beliefs and motivations that shaped those emotions; and finally, to make deliberate behavioral changes. The goal was health—emotional, moral, relational, and spiritual. But that goal has quietly, and sometimes not so quietly, shifted.

Today, the field of counseling is no longer primarily concerned with helping people grow or take responsibility for their lives. Instead, it has become preoccupied with affirming feelings, protecting emotions, and avoiding discomfort. Therapy, in its modern form, has transformed into a place where emotions are treated not as signals to be examined, but as truths to be revered. This seismic shift—from helping people confront and manage their feelings to validating and catering to them—has not made individuals healthier. It has made them fragile, self-focused, and increasingly dependent on therapy as a form of emotional anesthesia.

This chapter traces the evolution of that shift. It explores how we moved from insight-driven, growth-oriented therapy to a model that idolizes feelings. And it shows how the consequences of this change reach far beyond the therapy room—they are reshaping the way we parent, relate, teach, and live.

The Historical Roots of Counseling Psychology

To understand how modern therapy became so emotionally indulgent, we must begin with its foundational movements. Psychology, as a formal discipline, is relatively young—barely more than a century old. Yet within that time, its internal revolutions have redefined its purpose over and over again.

Psychoanalysis: Insight Through the Unconscious

In the early 1900s, Sigmund Freud pioneered psychoanalysis, a method of therapy that aimed to bring unconscious motivations into conscious awareness.[3] His method was slow and methodical. It required

---

[3] Corey, G. (2017). *Theory and Practice of Counseling and Psychotherapy* (10th ed.). Cengage Learning.

McLeod, J. (2013). *An Introduction to Counselling.* Open University Press.

introspection, dreams, dialogue, and deep exploration of childhood and sexual development. Freud believed that by uncovering hidden drives and past wounds, patients could gain insight—and through that insight, healing.

Though Freud's theories were flawed and sometimes outlandish, his focus on bringing unconscious patterns to light was foundational. It held to a basic assumption: people could grow. People could change. But first, they had to understand what drove them.

Behaviorism: Fix the Behavior, Forget the Feeling

By mid-century, Freud's influence waned, and a new school of thought emerged: behaviorism. Pioneers like John Watson and B.F. Skinner[4] rejected the murky introspection of psychoanalysis in favor of observable behavior and concrete change. Their methods were not interested in emotions, but in patterns. What mattered was not why a person felt the way they did, but whether they could behave differently.

This approach brought needed discipline to the field and proved remarkably effective in certain areas—particularly in treating phobias, compulsions, and addictions. But in

---

[4] Corey, G. (2017). *Theory and Practice of Counseling and Psychotherapy* (10th ed.). Cengage Learning.

McLeod, J. (2013). *An Introduction to Counselling*. Open University Press.

its zeal for outcomes, it dismissed the inner world of the client. Emotions, again, were sidelined.

Cognitive Therapy: Bridging Thought and Emotion

In the 1960s and 70s, a more balanced approach emerged. Aaron Beck and Albert Ellis introduced cognitive therapy, which connected emotions with thoughts. They taught that emotions are not independent forces—they're shaped by our beliefs, often distorted by irrational assumptions or past experiences. Therapy became a place to identify faulty thinking, challenge it, and replace it with truth.

This was a critical breakthrough. It gave people tools. It said, "Your emotions are real, but they are not always right. Let's look at what you're telling yourself, and see if it's true." This method respected feelings but did not idolize them. It sought both insight and action.

Humanistic Therapy: The Rise of the Self

Around the same time, another movement was quietly redefining the purpose of therapy. Humanistic psychologists like Carl Rogers and Abraham Maslow rejected the clinical distance of behaviorism and the pathology-focus of psychoanalysis. They believed in the innate goodness of people, the need for unconditional positive regard, and the pursuit of self-actualization.

Carl Rogers emphasized a non-directive, client-centered approach[5]. He encouraged therapists to accept all feelings as valid, to reflect back empathy without judgment. Maslow, meanwhile, proposed a hierarchy of needs, placing self-actualization—the fulfillment of one's potential—as the highest goal[6].

These ideas had noble intentions. They aimed to make therapy more humane. But they also introduced a quiet revolution: the shift from "understand and grow" to "feel and accept." Therapy was no longer about confronting difficult truths—it was about validating the self.

Melissa's Journey into the Feelings Spiral

Melissa, a 32-year-old teacher, began therapy to deal with chronic anxiety and failed relationships. Her therapist listened attentively, affirming her sadness, her frustration, and her recurring sense of being overlooked. Session after session, Melissa processed her emotions. She wept. She journaled. She unpacked her childhood. And yet, nothing changed.

After two years, Melissa was still in therapy. Her anxiety was worse. Her relationships were still crumbling. But now, she had a vocabulary for her emotions—"trauma," "toxic," "boundaries"—and a growing certainty that others were to blame for her pain. Her therapist, in

---

[5] Rogers, C. R. (1961). On Becoming a Person. Houghton Mifflin.

[6] Maslow, A. H. (1943). A Theory of Human Motivation. Psychological Review, 50(4), 370–396.

validating her emotional experience without ever challenging her patterns or inviting her into action, had become a co-conspirator in her stagnation.

The Decline of Insight-Based Therapy

Insight was once the goal of therapy. To see clearly. To understand oneself—not just emotionally, but cognitively and morally. The premise was simple: if I understand why I do what I do, I can begin to choose differently.

But as humanistic therapy gained ground, insight gave way to affirmation. Rogers' idea of unconditional positive regard—valuable in fostering safety—began to morph into unconditional emotional validation. Therapists, trained to avoid judgment, now feared correcting distorted thinking or confronting unhealthy behavior.

The "Feelings Are Truth" Fallacy

One of the most dangerous outcomes of this shift is the unspoken belief that "if I feel it, it must be true." This is emotional reasoning—a cognitive distortion that treats subjective feelings as objective facts. If I feel abandoned, then I must have been abandoned. If I feel disrespected, then someone must be disrespecting me.

In therapy sessions across the country, this fallacy reigns. And instead of being challenged, it is reinforced. The goal is no longer truth—it's comfort.

Tyler and the Weight of Unchallenged Emotion

Tyler, a 27-year-old graphic designer, came to therapy after a breakup. He told his therapist he felt "emotionally abused." His partner had ended the relationship after years of dysfunction. The therapist, concerned about Tyler's fragility, validated his feelings, affirmed his experience, and encouraged him to "honor his truth."

At no point did the therapist ask, "What was your role in this dynamic?" or "Is it possible your feelings, while real, may not reflect the full truth?" Tyler left therapy believing he was a victim. And he carried that belief into every future relationship.

The Influence of Cultural Movements on Therapy, Counterculture, and the Turn Against Restraint

The 1960s and 70s brought more than new music and fashion—they brought a radical rethinking of authority, morality, and discipline. The mantra became, "Do your own thing." Institutions were distrusted. Restraint was oppressive. Self-expression was sacred.

Therapy adapted. Rather than encouraging personal responsibility or moral self-examination, it began to echo the cultural call: "You be you." In this environment, the old virtues—discipline, humility, sacrifice—were replaced by self-love, emotional safety, and personal truth.

Trauma Culture and Emotional Fragility

The rise of trauma-informed care was a needed correction. It recognized that people with real trauma need real care. But over time, the definition of trauma expanded to include nearly every form of emotional discomfort. Now, nearly any emotional upset is treated as something sacred—not to be challenged, but to be honored.

Therapists, afraid of retraumatizing clients, tiptoe around truth. They affirm but do not confront. The result is clients who avoid growth in the name of emotional safety.

Postmodernism and the Death of Objective Reality

Postmodern thought injected a final toxin into the counseling field: the belief that there is no objective truth. Every perspective, every emotion, every identity is equally valid. No hierarchy of truth, no moral compass—just endless subjectivity.

Therapists trained in this worldview cannot guide—they can only affirm. To suggest that one emotional perspective might be wrong is to commit the unpardonable sin of "invalidating someone's experience."

The Three Stages of Healing in Therapy: A Guided Journey of Exploration, Insight, and Action

Counseling is at its most effective when it adheres to the well-established and evidence proven process available. Before we go any further in dissecting the problem we face in the modern application of professional counseling, let's stop and take a look at what effective counseling, which is biblically compatible by the way, looks like.

Healing through counseling is not an event—it's a *process*. And while every client's journey is unique, many follow a common pathway that unfolds in three essential stages: *Exploration, Insight,* and *Action*. These stages help organize the work of therapy, guiding clients from emotional chaos toward clarity, from self-sabotage toward stability.

Each stage builds on the last and requires the therapist to play a different but equally vital role—first as a compassionate witness, then as a guide and teacher, and finally as a coach and encourager. Below is a fuller understanding of how each stage functions and how a therapist supports the journey.

Stage One: Exploration – Understanding Your Emotions

What Happens in This Stage:

Exploration is about naming the internal experience. Many clients come into therapy overwhelmed by emotional patterns they don't understand. They might describe themselves as "too emotional," "numb," or "always on edge," but they can't explain why. In this first stage, the therapist creates a safe environment where clients can start identifying, expressing, and feeling their emotions without judgment.

The therapist listens carefully, often helping the client slow down and notice what they feel in their body, where they feel stuck, or what memories emerge when emotions arise. Gentle questions like, "What was that moment like for you?" or "Where do you feel that in your body?" help the client connect their emotions to past experiences, building awareness and trust in their own emotional signals.

How the Therapist Helps:

- Offers unconditional positive regard and emotional safety

- Reflects emotional content and body cues back to the client

- Helps develop emotional vocabulary (e.g., expanding beyond "mad" to include "resentful," "rejected," "abandoned")

- Uses tools like journaling, drawing, or imagery to help clients externalize internal states

- Tracks emotional themes and patterns across sessions for deeper exploration

Stage Two: Insight – Challenging and Correcting Faulty Beliefs

What Happens in This Stage:

Once the emotional experience is understood, therapy shifts toward clarity and meaning-making. The therapist now guides the client into examining the beliefs, assumptions, and interpretive lenses that shape their reactions. Many of these beliefs are subconscious, developed in childhood or trauma, and never questioned.

Clients begin to notice the stories they've been living under: *"I'm too much." "I'll be abandoned." "I don't matter."*

These beliefs often emerge naturally from the emotions explored in stage one. The therapist then introduces tools to dispute, reframe, and rewire these beliefs into healthier, more compassionate narratives.

How the Therapist Helps:

> Identifies cognitive distortions and gently challenges them
>
> Uses CBT, narrative therapy, or internal family systems to help examine belief systems
>
> Encourages curiosity over condemnation—"Where did you learn to believe that?" instead of "That's wrong."
>
> Reflects patterns between past experiences and current behavior
>
> Teaches reframing and offers new interpretations of painful memories

Stage Three: Action – Making Tangible Life Changes

What Happens in This Stage:

Now the client is ready to practice change. With emotional awareness and cognitive clarity in place, the therapist and client begin working on real-life behavior shifts—learning new communication strategies, setting boundaries, regulating in real time, or engaging in healthier relationships.

This stage is highly practical. The client begins testing new skills, taking relational risks, and building a life that reflects their healing rather than their trauma. The therapist helps the client troubleshoot setbacks, refine their strategies, and remain emotionally grounded.

How the Therapist Helps:

> Co-develops a personal healing plan with measurable goals
>
> Role-plays new behaviors (e.g., how to speak up, how to respond calmly in conflict)
>
> Reinforces progress and builds client confidence
>
> Introduces accountability tools (journals, check-ins, homework)
>
> Uses relapse-prevention strategies to maintain change

Melissa's Healing Journey Through the Three Stages

Melissa came to therapy overwhelmed and exhausted. She described herself as "emotionally volatile" and said she didn't trust herself in relationships. "One minute I'm fine," she said, "and the next I'm yelling, crying, or pulling away. I don't know what's wrong with me."

Stage One: Exploration

Her therapist began by helping Melissa track her emotions. They used a feelings wheel and explored how Melissa felt in different conflict moments. Melissa began to notice that her anger was often masking fear and sadness—feelings she never expressed as a child. In session, she shared a story of being left at daycare as a young girl and crying while her mother walked away. "I felt forgotten," she whispered. That memory brought up years of unspoken grief.

Over time, Melissa learned to pause when she felt triggered, name her emotions, and reflect on where they came from. For the first time, her emotions started to make sense.

Stage Two: Insight

As trust deepened, her therapist guided Melissa to explore the beliefs behind her emotions. Melissa realized she had lived under the belief: *"People always leave. If I don't hold them close, I'll be abandoned."* This belief caused her to cling tightly to others or shut down before they could reject her.

Together, they challenged the narrative. Her therapist helped her trace the belief back to childhood events—and to realize that not every goodbye was rejection. She began to reframe her thoughts: *"Not everyone will leave. Some people stay."*

This insight began to shift how she related to her current partner, opening space for healthier connection.

Stage Three: Action

Melissa was now ready to change how she behaved in real-time. She and her therapist created a trigger plan: when she felt anxious in her relationship, she would journal her thoughts, practice grounding techniques, and speak honestly with her partner rather than reacting with fear.

Her therapist role-played difficult conversations with her and encouraged her to join a faith-based support group for women. Slowly, Melissa started showing up differently in her relationships—with calm, confidence, and clarity.

She wasn't "fixed"—she was *freeing herself*. She no longer feared her emotions or avoided conflict. She knew what she felt, why she felt it, and how to respond with wisdom instead of panic.

Bringing It All Together: A Roadmap to Restoration

Therapy is not linear, but these three stages provide a scaffold for healing. Each one builds emotional muscle, helping the client move from surviving to thriving:

> **Exploration** creates awareness.
>
> **Insight** brings understanding.
>
> **Action** makes healing visible and lived.

Therapists support this journey by adapting their role to each stage—holding space in the beginning, challenging gently in the middle, and equipping courageously in the end.

For those who feel stuck in cycles of emotional pain, this process offers more than relief—it offers renewal. And with faith, grace, and the right guidance, healing is not only possible—it's already beginning.

The Shift to Perpetual Emotional Exploration

Therapy once followed the clear structure: *Exploration - Insight – Action*. But now, therapy stalls at the first stage.

Clients *explore emotions* endlessly, returning each week to process more feelings, relive more wounds, and seek more validation. Without insight or action, therapy becomes emotional indulgence—safe, comfortable, and completely ineffective.

The Dopamine Trap

Emotional validation feels good. It produces dopamine—a chemical reward for being seen, heard, and affirmed. But like any drug, it creates dependence. Clients become addicted to the feeling of being understood, without ever confronting the discomfort of change.

The Client Who Never Left

Angela started therapy after a divorce. Her therapist was warm, empathetic, and affirming. She felt seen. But every session was the same: reliving the pain, blaming her ex, and affirming her self-worth. There were no goals, no steps, no insight—just endless emotional processing.

Five years later, Angela was still in therapy. Still hurting. Still stuck. Therapy had become her emotional pacifier, not her path to healing.

Action and Resolution

Healthy therapy demands more than empathy. It requires courage—the courage to look inward, think critically, and act wisely. It invites clients to explore their emotions, yes—but not to live there. It calls them to insight, and then to action. True healing happens when we feel, think, and do.

Real Growth Through Real Therapy

Marcus came to therapy after years of broken relationships. His therapist, a Christian counselor, listened with compassion—but then asked hard questions. "What are you believing about yourself and others that keeps leading to this?" They explored Scripture. They identified lies. They built new habits.

It wasn't always comfortable. But over time, Marcus changed. Not because his feelings were always affirmed—but because they were examined in the light of truth.

When therapy becomes only about feelings, it stops being therapy. It becomes emotional indulgence dressed in clinical respectability. And as we will see, this is only the beginning. When the therapeutic world, influenced by postmodern ideology, also begins to reject objective morality and embrace moral relativism, the consequences become even more severe.

A Needed Correction, Not a Rejection

Let me take a moment to say something important. Emotional validation didn't just show up out of nowhere, and it didn't come from a bad place. It grew out of a real need. There was a time when people's pain was dismissed, when therapy was cold and clinical, and when those who were hurting felt ignored or misunderstood. Validation became a way to say, "What you feel matters." And that mattered a lot.

Advocacy-based therapy also had good intentions. It gave people a voice who had been silenced. It called attention to real injustices and helped the profession take a hard look at how power, culture, and trauma affect people's lives. That's not something I'm here to deny.

I remember working with a middle-aged woman named Dana who came to therapy after years in a rigid religious environment that treated all negative emotion as rebellion or weakness. For her, just being told that her sadness was valid—that it didn't make her faith defective—was healing in itself. She didn't need immediate insight or challenge; she needed a space where she was no longer punished for feeling. That space allowed her to trust again, and eventually, to grow. It was validation that opened the door—not as a destination, but as a beginning.

I also remember a powerful moment shared by my mentor during an overseas mission trip we shared in a third world country. He was counseling a local pastor and his wife in a group. They had recently lost their 11-year-old son in a freak accident at home. The tragedy alone was crushing—but what followed was even more devastating. Their church elders, well-meaning but deeply bound by religious performance, urged them not to grieve publicly. "Show the congregation your faith," they were told. "Let them see your confidence in your son's salvation." So they smiled. They quoted Scripture. They suppressed every tear. And in doing so, they buried not just their child—but their sorrow, their humanity, and their healing.

My mentor, with a presence both gentle and resolute, led a counseling session with the couple in front of their elders. He didn't confront their theology directly—he validated their pain. He named the unnatural silence around their grief. And slowly, almost imperceptibly at first, the tears began to fall. First the husband. Then the wife. Then the room. What followed wasn't emotional indulgence—it was holy ground. As the couple mourned their son openly, they also bore witness to a deeper truth: that Jesus weeps too. That our Savior, who knew the resurrection was coming, still paused to cry at Lazarus's tomb.

It was validation that unlocked that moment—not as an end point, but as a doorway. Feelings have merit and meaning when they are attended to in the proper order and for the right reasons. And in the right hands, the right presence, they can even become ministry.

This is why the early movement toward emotional attunement mattered. It gave permission to feel. It created safety where there had once been judgment. And for many people, it was the first time therapy felt like a refuge instead of an interrogation. These were necessary corrections to the cold, diagnosis-heavy models of previous decades.

But here's where I believe we've gone too far. In trying to make space for everyone's story, we stopped asking whether those stories are true—or helpful. In trying to make people feel safe, we stopped helping them get strong. In trying not to hurt anyone's feelings, we stopped saying the hard things that bring real change.

Validation is a good start. But if that's where therapy ends, people stay stuck. They don't grow. They feel heard, but not healed. And that's the problem I'm naming here—not that empathy is wrong, but that empathy without truth leaves people stranded.

Chapter Review: The Rise of Feelings-First Therapy

✦ A Better Way Forward

Therapy must go beyond comfort. While emotional validation can open doors, it should never become the destination. Growth requires more—clarity, challenge, and truth. As counselors and clients, we must learn to feel deeply, but also think wisely.

✦ Reflection & Response

- **Key Insight**: Modern therapy often prioritizes emotional validation over transformation. While emotions matter, they must not rule. Therapy should lead clients toward growth, not just comfort.
- **Challenge Question**: Where have I relied on emotional validation instead of pursuing growth?
- **Scripture Anchor**: Ephesians 4:15 – 'Speak the truth in love, growing in every way more and more like Christ.' (NIV)

In Chapter 3, *The Impact of Multicultural Eclecticism and Moral Relativism,* we will examine how multicultural eclecticism and the fear of offending have gutted therapy of its moral grounding—leaving people not only emotionally fragile, but spiritually lost.

40 Dr Chuck Carrington

Chapter 3:
The Impact of Multicultural Eclecticism and Moral Relativism
How Counseling Lost Its Moral Compass

When counseling abandons truth, it cannot help people change.

Therapy was once a process of guiding individuals toward mental, emotional, and moral health. The counselor helped clients confront unhealthy patterns, recognize faulty thinking, and take responsibility for their actions. But today, in many therapy rooms, that vision has all but disappeared.

Instead of pointing people toward universal truths—truths about personal responsibility, self-discipline, and moral integrity—modern therapy is often guided by a philosophy of multicultural eclecticism and moral relativism. These ideologies, shaped more by academic theory than clinical wisdom, have infused the counseling profession with an unwillingness to say what is good, right, or true. Worse, they have created a culture of emotional permissiveness, in which all beliefs are affirmed, all feelings are valid, and all perspectives are protected—no matter how damaging they may be.

This chapter traces the philosophical journey that led us here. It explores how therapy, shaped by the tides of postmodern academia and cultural pluralism, has lost its moral footing. And it reveals the consequences of this loss: the confusion, entitlement, and relational dysfunction that now plague both therapy and society.

1. How Academia Shaped Modern Counseling with Postmodern Ideology

Therapy does not exist in a vacuum. Like any profession, it is shaped by the prevailing ideas of the time. And in the last half-century, no idea has been more influential in reshaping the field of counseling than postmodernism.

Postmodernism and the Rejection of Truth

At its core, postmodernism is a philosophy that rejects objective truth. It teaches that reality is not discovered but constructed, that morality is not absolute but situational, and that meaning is not universal but personal.

This sounds harmless—maybe even enlightened. But in practice, postmodernism undercuts the very foundation of counseling. If there is no truth, there can be no guidance. If every perspective is equally valid, then even destructive behaviors must be accepted as part of a person's "lived experience."

When this thinking invaded academia in the late 20th century, it began reshaping how future therapists were trained. Rather than teaching them to guide clients toward truth, responsibility, and change, many counseling programs began emphasizing empathy without direction, affirmation without accountability, and "client-centeredness" without any moral center at all.

Multicultural Eclecticism: The Gateway to Moral Relativism

In the name of inclusivity, modern counseling embraced multiculturalism—not merely as a tool for understanding different backgrounds, but as a justification for moral neutrality. Therapists were taught to suspend judgment, affirm every worldview, and avoid imposing any values, even if the client's beliefs were clearly self-destructive.

At its best, multicultural awareness fosters respect and cross-cultural empathy. But in practice, it has often devolved into multicultural eclecticism—a grab-bag of therapeutic ideas pulled from various cultures, spiritualities, and ideologies with no unifying foundation.

This approach teaches that every culture's beliefs about family, morality, identity, and sexuality are equally valid, and that to challenge any of them is a form of "cultural oppression." But the truth is, not all beliefs promote health. Some damage people. Some distort reality. Some destroy relationships.

A Case of Cultural Confusion

Lena, a 24-year-old graduate student, came to therapy struggling with depression. Raised in a home that emphasized discipline, faith, and family loyalty, she had adopted a more progressive identity in college. Her therapist, trained in "affirmative therapy," encouraged her to reject "internalized oppression" and disconnect from her "restrictive upbringing."

Lena left therapy feeling validated—but more confused. The therapist never helped her examine whether her new values aligned with her core beliefs. Instead, they encouraged her to embrace autonomy at the expense of clarity. Lena's depression deepened, not because her upbringing was unhealthy, but because she was torn between her faith and a worldview she'd been taught not to question.

2. The Rejection of Objective Moral Frameworks in Therapeutic Practice

The new orthodoxy of counseling is moral neutrality. Therapists are no longer seen as guides, but as mirrors—reflecting whatever the client brings into the room without judgment or direction.

The Fear of Moral Judgment

Therapists are rightly taught to avoid condemning clients. But in today's therapy culture, even gentle moral guidance is seen as intrusive. A counselor who suggests that a client's sexual choices, parenting methods, or relational behaviors may be harmful is likely to be accused of imposing values.

In this environment, therapists are afraid to say what used to be obvious: that some behaviors are unhealthy, some beliefs are destructive, and some choices require correction—not affirmation.

Emotional Chaos Without Moral Anchors

Without moral guidance, therapy becomes an echo chamber of self-affirmation. Clients are told to "own their truth," but not to examine whether that truth aligns with reality or goodness. The result is a therapeutic paradox: people are encouraged to accept themselves without any call to improve themselves.

This moral vacuum fosters emotional confusion. People are told they can be anything, believe anything, feel anything—but they are never taught how to distinguish between truth and illusion, or between a feeling and a fact.

The Unchallenged Betrayer

David came to therapy after cheating on his wife. He felt guilt and shame—but also anger that his wife had "never understood him." His therapist, trying to create a safe space, affirmed David's pain and encouraged him to explore his unmet emotional needs.

What the therapist never did was challenge David's betrayal. The moral failure was never named. David left therapy with a clearer sense of his feelings, but no conviction about the harm he'd caused—or what it meant to make things right.

3. Fear of Traditional Values and the Demonization of Christian Normativity

One of the most troubling developments in modern therapy is its growing suspicion—if not outright hostility—toward Christian moral frameworks.

The Pathologizing of Biblical Beliefs

Therapists increasingly view religious convictions, especially those tied to traditional sexual ethics, gender roles, or marriage, as outdated and harmful. Clients who hold to biblical values are often subtly (or not so subtly) encouraged to "deconstruct" their beliefs.

In the name of psychological freedom, many therapists undermine faith-based convictions—suggesting that guilt, conviction, or a desire for self-control are signs of religious trauma rather than moral sensitivity.

Affirmative Therapy and Ideological Pressure

Affirmative therapy goes beyond neutrality. It requires therapists to affirm a client's identity, beliefs, or behaviors without question—even if those beliefs conflict with reality, biblical values, or long-term health. This approach, rooted in activist ideologies, leaves no room for moral conversation.

For the Christian client seeking therapy, this creates an impossible choice: embrace a therapist who may reject their core convictions or settle for self-help books and church counseling, which are often dismissed by the clinical community.

A Christian Couple in Crisis

James and Abigail, a Christian couple in their forties, sought marital counseling for intimacy issues. They explained to the therapist that their faith shaped their view of marriage, sexuality, and forgiveness. The therapist, trained in "non-directive practice," listened—but quickly began challenging their beliefs.

She encouraged Abigail to explore whether "traditional gender roles" were holding her back, and asked James if his commitment to "marital purity" was rooted in "patriarchal control." The therapist wasn't neutral. She was actively dismantling the couple's convictions.

James and Abigail left after three sessions—feeling not helped, but attacked.

4. The Loss of Moral Guidance in Favor of Personal Self-Affirmation

The new goal of therapy is not transformation—it's affirmation. The client's emotions are treated as the highest authority. Moral guidance is considered oppressive. And personal responsibility is quietly replaced with self-justification.

Therapy as Emotional Indulgence

Therapists now hesitate to correct, guide, or challenge. Their job is to "hold space" for clients—to witness, to empathize, but not to lead. This creates a therapeutic culture where people feel good about themselves but make little progress in their lives.

Emotional strength, like physical strength, is built through discomfort. But modern therapy, in its quest for safety, shields clients from discomfort—leaving them emotionally weak.

The Rise of Narcissism

When therapy validates every feeling and affirms every belief, clients begin to see themselves as the center of reality. They are not challenged to see how their choices affect others. They are not called to sacrifice, to serve, or to submit to any higher truth. Their inner world becomes the only world that matters.

This is how therapy, intended to heal, ends up cultivating narcissism.

The Me-First Mentality

Samantha, a young professional, was in therapy to process her dissatisfaction with life. She often spoke about how others failed to meet her expectations—her friends weren't affirming enough, her parents didn't understand her, her boss didn't appreciate her.

Her therapist empathized deeply, reinforcing her right to feel frustrated. But over time, Samantha's resentment grew. She never asked if her expectations were fair, or if she might need to adjust her view of others. Therapy confirmed her feelings, but never challenged her entitlement.

Action and Resolution: Rediscovering Moral Clarity in Counseling

Therapy must return to truth. Not as dogma, but as direction. Counselors do not need to impose a worldview—but they must be willing to say: "This behavior is harmful," or "That belief is not based in reality," or "You have the power to choose differently."

Healthy therapy requires a moral framework. It requires courage. It requires the humility to say: "Your feelings are valid—but they are not always right. Let's explore them. Let's examine them. Let's bring them into the light."

Counseling That Honors Truth

Ben, a 29-year-old struggling with pornography addiction, found a Christian counselor who listened, affirmed his pain, but also challenged his thinking. The counselor helped Ben see how his habits were not just a personal problem but a spiritual and relational one.

Together, they worked through Scripture, cognitive-behavioral tools, and accountability structures. It wasn't always easy. But Ben experienced change—not because he was affirmed, but because he was confronted with truth, and invited to live differently.

Therapy that loses its moral compass cannot heal. It can affirm. It can comfort. But it cannot change lives.

As we've seen, multicultural eclecticism and moral relativism have eroded the foundation of counseling. What remains is not guidance, but confusion. Not resilience, but fragility. Not truth, but emotional indulgence.

But this is not the end. The damage doesn't stop with relativism—it continues as therapy becomes a tool for activism. In the next chapter, we'll explore how the counseling profession has gone beyond moral neutrality to become an engine for ideological advocacy. When therapy promotes politics instead of personal healing, the results are even more dangerous.

Chapter Review: The Loss of Moral Frameworks in Modern Therapy

✦ A Better Way Forward

Without a moral compass, counseling becomes a wandering journey. People need more than empathy—they need direction. Reclaiming a shared framework of truth doesn't limit healing; it empowers it.

✦ Reflection & Response

- **Key Insight**: Counseling without a moral compass can leave clients adrift. A clear framework of truth

provides direction and protects against self-justification.
- **Challenge Question**: How does a lack of moral structure in therapy affect my ability to grow?
- **Scripture Anchor**: Proverbs 14:12 – 'There is a way that seems right to a man, but its end is the way to death.'

In Chapter 4: *The Advocacy Problem in Professional Counseling,* we'll uncover how therapy has become a vehicle not just for emotional affirmation—but for cultural and political indoctrination.

Chapter 4:
The Advocacy Problem in Professional Counseling
When Therapy Becomes Ideology

Therapy used to be a place for healing.

It was a sacred space—quiet, respectful, and intentional. People entered the counseling room burdened with pain, confusion, fear, or failure. They left with clarity, insight, and the beginning of hope. The counselor was not a guru, not a fixer, not a friend—but a guide. Their role was to help the client understand themselves, think critically, and chart a path forward. And always, it was the client's path—not the therapist's agenda.

But that's changing.

Modern therapy is no longer content to be neutral. Instead, it has become a platform for activism. Increasingly, counseling is used to promote social justice ideology, reinforce political narratives, and reshape clients' worldviews in alignment with progressive values. Therapy has drifted from its core mission—personal healing—and become a stage for cultural advocacy.

This chapter examines the consequences of this shift: how the counseling profession has allowed advocacy to replace neutrality, how social justice ideology now saturates therapy, and how clients are often led away from personal responsibility toward political identity. In doing so, the field has compromised its integrity and lost its ability to genuinely help people grow.

1. The Shift from Neutral Guidance to Political and Cultural Activism

The Traditional Role of Counselors as Neutral Guides

For most of its history, professional counseling embraced the role of neutral guidance. Therapists were taught to listen without judgment, reflect without bias, and help clients discover their own truth through insight and action. While personal values were never absent, they were held with humility. The counselor was a mirror—not a mouthpiece.

This neutrality allowed clients to explore their thoughts and emotions honestly. They weren't pressured to conform. They weren't told what to believe. Instead, they were invited to think. A good therapist helped a client discover not just how they felt, but *why*—and then, what to do about it.

But neutrality is no longer in vogue.

The Rise of Advocacy Counseling

In the last two decades, many counselor education programs have embraced a new model: the counselor not as guide, but as advocate. Under the banner of social justice, therapists are now encouraged to serve as agents of change—to stand with the oppressed, challenge systems of inequality, and help clients "find their voice" by aligning with certain ideological beliefs.

At first glance, this seems compassionate. After all, who doesn't want to stand with the hurting? But beneath the surface, something dangerous is happening. Counselors are no longer merely offering support—they are shaping belief. Therapy becomes less about personal growth and more about political conformity.

When the Counselor Becomes the Preacher

Maria, a 19-year-old college student, sought therapy after a traumatic breakup. She hoped to work through her sadness, her trust issues, and her questions about self-worth. But her therapist quickly shifted the conversation.

"You need to understand," the therapist said, "how much patriarchy affects your relationships. The way men dominate women… it's part of the system." Session after session, Maria was taught that her pain wasn't just personal—it was political.

Eventually, Maria stopped asking about her own behavior. She stopped wondering what she could learn or change. The therapist had given her an identity—as a victim of cultural oppression—and Maria accepted it. She left therapy feeling affirmed, but disempowered.

Objectivity Undermined by Ideological Assumptions

The new advocacy model centers around group identity. Counselors are taught to see clients not as individuals, but as members of intersecting systems of privilege and oppression. Race, gender, sexuality, and socioeconomic status become the primary lenses through which struggles are interpreted.

This lens promotes external blame rather than internal reflection. Clients are encouraged to view their pain as the result of systemic injustice rather than personal responsibility. The result is therapy that reinforces helplessness instead of promoting growth.

2. The Introduction of "Therapeutic Social Justice"

Social Justice Counseling Education

Today's counselor education programs frequently train students to become "agents of social change." Many graduate programs now require coursework in multicultural competence and social justice advocacy. These are not inherently problematic goals. Understanding cultural context can be valuable in therapy. But when "cultural competence" becomes code for ideological compliance, therapy is no longer a place for discovery—it becomes a classroom for indoctrination.

Terms like "power dynamics," "privilege," and "systemic oppression" have become therapeutic dogma. Therapists are told to help clients understand how they are "oppressed" by systems, rather than how they may be misinterpreting their circumstances or mismanaging their emotions.

Ideologically Driven Therapy

Ideological therapy doesn't invite clients to think critically. It tells them what to believe. It presents a narrow framework of acceptable conclusions: If you're hurting, it must be someone else's fault. If you're anxious, it's because of oppression. If you're angry, it's righteous indignation against injustice.

This model may offer short-term relief, but it stunts emotional maturity. It discourages introspection. It trains clients to see the world in terms of enemies and allies, power and powerlessness, oppression and resistance—rather than as a complex interplay of personal choices, relationships, and beliefs.

A Young Man in Therapy

Jordan, a 25-year-old teacher, entered therapy for depression. He was grieving the recent death of his father, navigating a career change, and struggling with anger. His therapist quickly introduced the concept of "racialized trauma."

Jordan, who was biracial, had not mentioned race as a central issue. But the therapist pressed the theme, suggesting his anger might stem from "internalized oppression" and systemic racism.

Jordan left therapy confused. He didn't feel seen. His story had been reinterpreted through a lens he didn't relate to. What he needed was help understanding his grief and his own emotional history. What he received was a politicized narrative.

Emotional Growth Replaced with Identity Politics

When therapy becomes activism, personal growth is replaced by collective ideology. Clients are told how to see the world. They are praised when they affirm the narrative. And they are quietly corrected when they stray from it.

Rather than empowering individuals to change themselves, therapy becomes a platform for changing society—one client at a time.

3. How Advocacy-Based Therapy Undermines Genuine Self-Awareness

The Death of Critical Thinking

Traditional therapy was based on helping clients question themselves—examining thoughts, challenging assumptions, and reframing perspectives. But advocacy-based therapy often reverses that process. Clients are taught to question the world, but never themselves. Their emotions are validated, but never evaluated. Their assumptions are affirmed, but never scrutinized.

In this model, disagreement with the dominant ideology is seen as ignorance—or worse, bigotry. The client who questions whether systemic forces are truly to blame may be labeled "uninformed." Exploration is discouraged. Conformity is rewarded.

A Woman Seeking Help

Tasha, a 38-year-old mother, sought counseling to manage work stress and marital conflict. She was a devout Christian and expressed a desire to make her marriage work through forgiveness, communication, and faith.

Her therapist, uncomfortable with Tasha's values, encouraged her to focus on "self-actualization" and "breaking free" from patriarchal expectations. Suggestions of prayer, grace, or reconciliation were met with skepticism.

Tasha left therapy feeling confused and ashamed. She hadn't been helped—she had been judged. Her values weren't honored—they were dismantled.

Victimhood Over Responsibility

One of the great dangers of ideology-driven therapy is its tendency to reinforce victimhood. Rather than helping clients ask, "What can I change?" they are taught to ask, "Who is doing this to me?" Instead of owning their choices, they are encouraged to seek external villains. This makes therapy feel empowering—but it is false power.

True power comes from responsibility. When we take ownership of our thoughts, emotions, and behaviors, we grow. When we blame others, we stagnate.

4. Examples of Ideological Influence in Professional Counseling Organizations

The ACA and the Push for Advocacy

The American Counseling Association (ACA), once a standard-bearer of professional ethics, now openly advocates for political causes. Its publications, conferences, and code of ethics increasingly reflect progressive ideology—particularly regarding race, gender, and sexuality.

While some of these efforts may be well-intentioned, they have led to the marginalization of counselors who hold different views. Faith-based counselors, for example, often feel pressured to conform to the ACA's ideology or risk professional consequences.

Affirmative Therapy vs. Exploratory Counseling

Nowhere is this more evident than in the area of gender identity. Once, therapy invited clients to explore their sense of self, reflect on identity, and consider multiple paths forward. Today, "affirmative therapy" means the therapist must validate the client's self-declared identity—without question.

This removes the possibility of careful exploration. A young person experiencing confusion is given affirmation, not investigation. And counselors who take a slower, more reflective approach may be accused of doing harm.

The Silencing of Dissent

Therapists who dissent from the ideological orthodoxy risk being silenced. Some have lost licenses, jobs, or educational opportunities because they refused to affirm every identity, or because they held to religious convictions.

The result is a profession increasingly dominated by a single worldview. This is not therapeutic diversity. It is ideological conformity.

A Counselor Under Pressure

Mark, a licensed therapist in his early 50s, worked with youth and families for over two decades. He held traditional Christian beliefs and practiced with compassion and integrity.

After declining to affirm a teenager's sudden transgender identification without further exploration, Mark was reported. Though he never imposed his views, and always acted with care, he was removed from his counseling program as "non-compliant with inclusive practices."

Mark's story is not unique. Many counselors now practice in fear—afraid that ethical, thoughtful approaches will be seen as ideological resistance.

Action and Resolution: Reclaiming Therapy as a Path to Healing

Therapy must return to its purpose: helping individuals grow. This means listening, empathizing, and guiding—but not preaching. It means allowing clients to explore, to struggle, and to find answers that are both emotionally honest and morally grounded.

Counselors must have the courage to step back from activism and step into the sacred work of helping people become whole. They must create space for different worldviews, respect personal convictions, and reject the impulse to prescribe ideology.

A Different Kind of Therapy

Rachel, a 45-year-old divorcee, was filled with bitterness and grief. Her therapist listened patiently. But after hearing her story, he asked gently, "What do you think forgiveness might look like?" At first, Rachel was offended. But over time, she began to open.

That question didn't affirm her rage. It didn't endorse victimhood. But it planted a seed. Therapy became a journey—not of affirmation, but transformation. Rachel changed—not because she aligned with a social cause, but because she confronted her heart.

Therapy is no longer a neutral space for growth. It has become a battleground of ideologies. And in the name of justice, it has abandoned truth. But as we will see, this ideological advocacy is not the only threat to emotional health. Even more dangerous is the belief that our emotions themselves are truth.

Chapter Review: Ideological Capture and Activism in Counseling

✦ A Better Way Forward

When ideology overtakes integrity in the counseling room, healing is replaced by persuasion. The counselor's job is not to convince, but to companion—with clarity and humility. Clients need guides, not activists.

✦ Reflection & Response

- **Key Insight**: Activist counseling trades objectivity for ideology. When counselors become advocates instead of guides, therapy turns into persuasion, not healing.
- **Challenge Question**: When have I experienced ideology overtaking truth in a helping relationship?
- **Scripture Anchor**: Colossians 2:8 – 'See to it that no one takes you captive through hollow and deceptive philosophy.'

In Chapter 5: *Emotional Reasoning and the Death of Objective Truth*, we'll explore how elevating feelings above facts has led to cognitive distortions, entitlement, and emotional fragility. If emotions become the ultimate authority, how can we ever find truth—or healing?

Chapter 5: Emotional Reasoning and the Death of Objective Truth

When Feelings Replace Facts, Growth Stops

We are living in an age where feelings are king.

In this new emotional empire, therapy no longer helps people understand and govern their emotions—it tells them that their emotions are the final authority. "If you feel it, it must be true," has become the mantra of both culture and counseling. And with that simple distortion, a generation has been trained to abandon objective reality in favor of emotional reasoning.

Emotional reasoning—the belief that your emotions define truth—is a dangerous cognitive distortion. It warps identity, poisons relationships, and stifles growth. And instead of challenging it, modern therapy has too often reinforced it.

This chapter explores how therapy has lost its grip on truth. By prioritizing emotional validation over cognitive challenge, the field has promoted a culture of hypersensitivity, victimhood, and relational dysfunction. The result is a society where people are encouraged to interpret life not through wisdom, but through the volatile lens of their feelings. What was once a path to healing has become a tunnel of self-justification and emotional indulgence.

1. The Dangers of Elevating Feelings Above Logic and Facts

What Is Emotional Reasoning?

Emotional reasoning is the cognitive distortion that equates feelings with facts. If I feel anxious, I must be in danger. If I feel disrespected, someone must have disrespected me. If I feel worthless, I must be worthless.

This distortion short-circuits rational evaluation. It disconnects people from the disciplines of thinking, discernment, and truth-seeking. Instead of asking, "Is this belief accurate?", clients are taught to ask, "How does this make me feel?" And the more therapy centers around this question, the less it helps.

From Cognitive Therapy to Emotional Validation

Cognitive-behavioral therapy (CBT), once the gold standard in evidence-based treatment, taught clients to challenge irrational beliefs. It trained people to observe their feelings, test their assumptions, and build emotional strength through truth.

But in many therapy circles today, cognitive restructuring has been pushed aside in favor of emotional validation. The goal is no longer to ask, "Is this belief based in truth?" but rather, "How can I support this belief because you feel it?"

This shift has had disastrous consequences.

Casey's Panic Loop

Casey, a 33-year-old accountant, came to therapy for panic attacks. She feared losing control, feared embarrassment, feared everything going wrong. In CBT, her therapist might have helped her test those fears, evaluate their basis, and develop calming strategies.

But her therapist, trained in emotion-centered therapy, instead focused on affirming Casey's experience. "Your fear makes sense. Let's explore it." Session after session, they dug deeper into Casey's feelings—but never challenged them.

Months later, Casey's panic attacks were worse. Her feelings had been explored, but never exposed to truth.

How This Shift Increases Emotional Fragility

When emotions are never questioned, they grow unchecked. Research shows that individuals who rely heavily on emotional reasoning report higher levels of anxiety and depression. Why? Because the more they interpret the world through emotion, the more distorted that world becomes.

If someone constantly believes they are being mistreated, ignored, or endangered—without evaluating the facts—emotional exhaustion follows. Without truth, there is no anchor. And therapy, meant to be the place where falsehoods are confronted, becomes the echo chamber that reinforces them.

2. How Emotional Reasoning Leads to Entitlement and Victim Mentality

Emotional Fragility: The New Normal

In a world ruled by feelings, strength is suspect. Endurance is viewed as repression. And emotional fragility becomes a sign of authenticity. If someone is offended, we are told to accommodate. If someone feels unsafe, we must remove the "trigger."

But real life doesn't work that way.

Emotional fragility makes everyday life unbearable. When people are trained to interpret discomfort as danger, they cannot handle disagreement, correction, or growth. They break under pressure and blame others for the shards.

The "Wounded" Intern

Logan, a 24-year-old intern at a nonprofit, overheard a coworker disagreeing with a political view he held. Feeling hurt, Logan reported the coworker to HR, claiming the disagreement had created a "hostile environment."

Instead of exploring why the comment offended him or considering a different perspective, Logan was affirmed by a culture that equates discomfort with harm. Emotional reasoning told him: *If I feel hurt, someone must have wronged me.*

The organization, afraid of controversy, reassigned the coworker. Logan felt vindicated—but not stronger.

Safe Spaces and the Shrinking Mind

"Safe space" is a common term in education and counseling, originally meant to create room for openness. But it has morphed into a demand: nothing must ever feel unsafe.

This expectation conditions people to avoid difficulty rather than grow through it. Emotional maturity is never forged in comfort. It requires friction—learning how to think in the presence of tension. But therapy that shields people from conflict trains them for weakness.

Victimhood: A Psychological Dead End

Emotional reasoning is the fuel of the victim mindset. If your feelings are always justified, then someone else must always be to blame. Instead of asking, "What can I learn?", the emotionally reasoned mind asks, "Who did this to me?"

Therapy that feeds this cycle disables clients. They stop seeking growth. They seek vindication.

3. The Psychological Consequences of Avoiding Cognitive Restructuring

Emotional Reasoning and the Loss of Identity

When people are taught that their emotions define who they are, they become trapped in a distorted identity. If I feel anxious, I *am* an anxious person. If I feel worthless, I *am* unlovable. These statements become self-fulfilling.

This is why therapy must return to cognitive restructuring. People need to be taught that feelings are not facts. They are indicators, not dictators. They must be examined, not obeyed.

The Woman Who Couldn't Forgive Herself

Emily had an abortion in her early 20s. Years later, she still struggled with guilt and shame. Her therapist encouraged her to "trust her inner wisdom" and "honor her truth." But Emily's feelings of guilt never subsided.

She didn't need affirmation. She needed truth—about sin, grace, forgiveness, and healing. But therapy never gave her a framework for confronting her actions or finding peace.

She remained stuck—because no one helped her look beyond her feelings to find hope in something greater.

Emotional Reasoning Destroys Relationships

Relationships thrive on clarity, humility, and self-regulation. But when people believe that their emotions are always correct, conflict becomes impossible to resolve.

If I feel disrespected, then you must have disrespected me. No amount of evidence, apologies, or reasoning matters. Feelings have become facts. Truth is irrelevant.

This creates a relational nightmare: emotional manipulation, chronic misunderstandings, and an inability to forgive.

The Societal Collapse of Dialogue

On a societal scale, emotional reasoning has silenced dialogue. If someone's opinion causes discomfort, they are canceled. If a speaker presents facts that offend, they are shouted down.

Civil disagreement has become impossible because people now view contradiction as harm. And as a result, our society is intellectually and emotionally regressing.

4. The Role of Therapy in Reinforcing Rather Than Challenging Emotions

The Over-Validation Trap

Validation has its place in therapy. People need to be heard. But when validation becomes the sole goal, therapy reinforces emotional reasoning. "Your feelings are valid" is true in the sense that emotions are real—but it is not always true that the beliefs behind them are accurate.

Validation must be paired with challenge. "I hear you. Now let's look at whether that thought is true." That is what leads to change.

The Therapist Who Couldn't Say No

Brent, a college student, came to therapy after a breakup. He claimed his partner had "emotionally abused" him by asking for space. His therapist, without any examination, affirmed Brent's feelings.

Over time, Brent became more resentful, more cynical, and more self-righteous. Therapy had validated his feelings—but never invited him to question his expectations or recognize his own role.

He left therapy convinced of his victimhood—and unable to maintain healthy relationships.

The Loss of Objective Standards

Therapy was once anchored in objective psychological principles. Clients were helped to align their lives with reality. But the rise of moral and epistemological relativism has gutted that foundation.

Now, the goal is comfort, not change. And comfort alone never produces health.

Why Therapists Fear Cognitive Challenge

Many therapists are afraid to challenge clients because of cultural pressure. Confronting faulty thinking is viewed as "judgmental" or "unsafe." But real therapy *must* confront. Not cruelly, but clearly.

Discomfort is not abuse. Correction is not oppression. And without cognitive challenge, there is no transformation—only emotional indulgence.

Action and Resolution: Returning to Truth-Based Healing

The path forward is not complicated. It is the path therapy once followed:

- **Validate emotions**—yes.
- **Challenge thoughts**—always.
- **Pursue truth**—unflinchingly.

People need help to separate what they feel from what is real. They need frameworks to evaluate their emotions, not just explore them. They need therapists with the courage to ask: "Is this belief true? Is this emotion guiding you toward life or keeping you stuck?"

Freedom Through Truth

Caleb, a 40-year-old entrepreneur, came to therapy paralyzed by guilt after a failed business venture. He said, "I feel like I'm a failure." His therapist replied, "Let's look at that. What defines failure?"

Together, they unpacked his beliefs, corrected his assumptions, and rebuilt his identity—not on emotions, but on truth.

Caleb didn't leave therapy with warm feelings. He left with something better: clarity, responsibility, and strength.

Therapy that prioritizes feelings over facts fails its clients. It reinforces weakness, promotes confusion, and undermines resilience. Emotional reasoning must be named, challenged, and replaced with truth-based thinking.

But the damage doesn't stop in the therapy office. The rise of emotional reasoning has shaped how we parent, how we relate, and how we raise boys into men.

Chapter Review: Emotional Reasoning and the Collapse of Truth

✦ A Better Way Forward

Our emotions are real, but they are not rulers. If we elevate feelings above facts, we lose our grip on growth. Therapy that heals must invite us to question, test, and transform our emotional responses with truth.

✦ Reflection & Response

- **Key Insight**: Emotional reasoning is seductive but misleading. Feelings are real, but they are not always true. Learning to evaluate emotions through the lens of truth restores integrity.
- **Challenge Question**: In what areas do I trust my feelings more than I should?
- **Scripture Anchor**: Psalm 26:2 – 'Test me, Lord, and try me, examine my heart and my mind.'

In Chapter 6: *Gentle Parenting, Weak Men, and Me-First Relationships*, we'll examine how therapy's emotional-centric model has redefined parenting styles, emasculated masculine strength, and encouraged self-centered relationship dynamics that prioritize feelings over commitment, growth, and love.

Chapter 6:
Gentle Parenting, Weak Men, and Me-First Relationships

How Therapy Has Undermined Resilience, Masculinity, and Commitment

In our therapeutic age, we've replaced strength with sensitivity, discipline with dialogue, and commitment with comfort. The results are evident—and devastating.

Children crumble under pressure, men shrink back from leadership, and relationships collapse under the weight of unmet expectations. What once defined human maturity—emotional regulation, sacrificial love, and personal responsibility—has been quietly replaced by emotional fragility, entitlement, and a culture of self-first thinking. At the center of this shift is therapy—not therapy as it was meant to be, but therapy as it has become: a practice more concerned with feelings than with growth, more affirming than transforming.

This chapter examines how the modern therapeutic mindset shaped parenting, masculinity, and relationships.

From gentle parenting models that over validate children's feelings, to a cultural war on masculine strength, to relationships reimagined as self-care partnerships—we will trace how therapy's influence, when untethered from truth, has weakened the very structures that sustain a healthy society.

1. How Therapy-Influenced Parenting Models Encourage Emotional Fragility

The Rise of Gentle Parenting

Today's most popular parenting advice is saturated with therapeutic language: validate every feeling, avoid punishment, allow children to express all emotions freely. This model, often referred to as "gentle parenting," aims to create emotionally safe homes. And on the surface, this seems wise—who wouldn't want to raise emotionally aware children?

But beneath this good intention lies a serious flaw: in rejecting structure and discipline, these models train children to believe that their emotions are the highest authority. Parents are taught not to correct but to mirror. Not to guide, but to affirm. The child's emotions become the compass—and the adult becomes the weather vane, spinning in response.

The Grocery Store Meltdown

Amanda stood in the cereal aisle as her 4-year-old screamed uncontrollably. "I want the chocolate one!" he yelled. Other shoppers looked on with concern—or judgment. Amanda crouched beside him and softly said, "I understand you're disappointed. You feel sad. That's okay."

After five minutes of affirming his emotions, the tantrum had not ceased. Amanda had been taught never to say "no" harshly, never to discipline without explanation. But the child wasn't looking for validation—he needed a boundary.

The Dangers of Over-Validation

Validation is important—but when overused or misapplied, it conditions children to believe their feelings should never be challenged. A child who is never told "no" or corrected firmly will grow up emotionally fragile, unable to tolerate frustration or delay.

Emotions are real—but they are not always right. When parenting models affirm every feeling without helping the child interpret or manage it, they fail to teach one of life's most essential lessons: your feelings matter, but they do not define reality.

The Consequences of Eliminating Discipline

In today's cultural climate, discipline is often misunderstood as harsh or authoritarian. But biblically and psychologically, discipline is love. "Whom the Lord loves He disciplines," writes the author of Hebrews. A parent who lovingly corrects is doing more than managing behavior—they are shaping character.

When discipline is removed, children become emotionally chaotic. They grow into adults who cannot self-regulate, handle disappointment, or take responsibility. The result? A fragile generation raised on the false promise that their emotions should always be affirmed—and never challenged.

2. The Decline of Masculine Resilience Due to Therapeutic Passivity

The Therapeutic Attack on Masculinity

For generations, masculinity meant something noble: strength under control, courage in adversity, leadership with humility, and responsibility without complaint. But in recent decades, these traits have been recast as "toxic."

Therapy, increasingly shaped by feminist and postmodern frameworks, has often painted traditional masculinity as inherently oppressive. Men are told to abandon stoicism, suppress competitiveness, and "get in touch" with their feelings. While emotional awareness has value, the message has shifted from *balance* to *abandonment*—abandon what made men strong and replace it with sensitivity.

The Lost Husband

Brian, a 42-year-old husband and father of three, came to therapy confused and frustrated. He was told by his wife to "be more emotional," "more present," "more vulnerable." He had tried, but the more he opened up, the more lost he felt.

His therapist encouraged more emotional expression, less decision-making, and more focus on "his own needs." Brian became more self-focused—but less effective. His wife grew resentful. She didn't want a man lost in his own emotional process. She wanted a husband who would lead with love and courage.

How Therapy Has Weakened Men's Role as Leaders

True masculinity is not aggression or dominance—it is servant leadership. It is the willingness to bear burdens, make sacrifices, and take responsibility. But therapy's passive model of manhood has encouraged many men to turn inward rather than step up.

Instead of equipping men to lead with integrity, modern counseling often reinforces introspection without action. This has led to relational breakdowns, as men retreat from the very challenges they were designed to confront.

The Societal Cost of Therapeutic Masculinity

A generation of young men has now grown up confused about who they are and what they are for. Taught to mistrust their instincts and suppress their strengths, many drift into passivity, addiction, and relational disengagement.

We see the results: declining marriage rates, rising male depression, academic underperformance, and disengagement from fatherhood. In trying to avoid the pitfalls of toxic masculinity, society has embraced an equally dangerous extreme—emasculation by therapeutic passivity.

3. The Promotion of Self-Focused Relationships Over Mutual Sacrifice

From Duty to Personal Happiness

Relationships once thrived on shared duty, mutual sacrifice, and covenantal commitment. But in the therapy-informed age, marriage is no longer viewed as a sacred bond—but as a vehicle for personal fulfillment.

When people no longer feel "happy" or "seen," they are told to walk away. If a partner no longer "meets their needs," the relationship is viewed as invalid. Feelings are the metric. And when feelings fade, so does commitment.

The Disillusioned Wife

Rachel had been married for eight years. Her husband was faithful, hard-working, and kind—but emotionally distant. She went to therapy to explore her unhappiness. Instead of helping her work through the disappointment, her therapist asked, "Do you feel emotionally fulfilled?"

Rachel replied, "Not really."

"Then maybe you've outgrown this relationship," her therapist said.

No exploration of what commitment meant. No encouragement to work through difficulty. Just a license to leave.

Therapy's Self-First Mindset

Self-care, once a helpful concept, has been weaponized into a philosophy of self-first. While emotional health is vital, the overemphasis on "what I need" has replaced "what I give."

In this model, love is not a commitment to serve—it is a feeling to be sustained. Partners become consumers. Relationships are evaluated like products: "Is this meeting my needs?"

But true love is not found in constant satisfaction—it is forged in sacrificial giving.

The Rise of Consumer Relationships

Many modern relationships resemble contracts, not covenants. Each person asks, "What do I get from this?" rather than "How can I love well here?"

Therapy that encourages people to seek only what they deserve, without emphasizing what they must give, contributes to a relational landscape marked by transience, resentment, and immaturity.

4. How Therapeutic Ideology Discourages Personal Responsibility in Relationships

Toxicity Labels and the Death of Introspection

One of the most concerning trends in therapy is the explosion of psychological labels used not diagnostically—but defensively. Words like "narcissist," "gaslighting," and "toxic" are now thrown around casually, often to justify exits rather than foster insight.

While real abuse exists, the overuse of these terms shuts down conversation. Instead of asking, "How can I grow in this?", people ask, "How is this person harming me?"

The Misdiagnosed Boyfriend

Claire ended her two-year relationship after a heated argument. Her therapist asked if she had considered that her boyfriend might be narcissistic. Claire had never thought so before—but the suggestion gave her a new lens.

Suddenly, all his flaws became evidence. His occasional forgetfulness? Gaslighting. His stress at work? Emotional unavailability. Within weeks, Claire was not only justified in ending the relationship—she saw herself as having escaped an abuser.

No one asked if Claire had been demanding, or whether reconciliation was possible. The diagnosis replaced the dialogue.

Therapy-Informed Breakups

Many people now go to therapy not to *save* their relationships—but to be *affirmed* in ending them. Counselors, trained in client-centered models, are often hesitant to challenge their client's narratives. But without challenge, therapy becomes validation—not transformation.

While some relationships should end, many could be healed. But healing requires responsibility. It requires two people asking, "What can I do differently?"—not one person being told, "You deserve better."

Returning to Responsibility and Sacrifice

Relationships are hard. They require effort, humility, and endurance. Therapy must recapture its calling to help people stay—not just leave. It must champion forgiveness, conflict resolution, and self-sacrifice.

Without this, relationships will continue to collapse under the weight of unmet expectations and self-focused demands.

Action and Resolution: Rebuilding the Foundations of Strength, Sacrifice, and Resilience

The way back is not complex—but it is costly. We must return to biblical and psychological truths:

- **Parenting** requires love *and* discipline.
- **Masculinity** must be reclaimed as strength in service.
- **Relationships** must be rooted in covenant, not comfort.

Therapy must once again teach that resilience is not repression, that leadership is not domination, and that love is not entitlement—it is self-giving.

A Father Who Chose Strength

Darren, a father of two teenage boys, was tired of chaos. His home felt out of control—rules weren't followed, emotions ruled the day, and respect was fading. He started reading Scripture again. He went to a counselor who believed in accountability.

He made changes. He started leading with strength and tenderness. He corrected without yelling. He loved without coddling. Slowly, the tone of his home changed.

He wasn't just raising boys. He was raising men.

Therapy, when guided by truth, can build strong families, resilient men, and enduring relationships. But when it elevates emotion above discipline, self above sacrifice, and feelings above facts—it tears these structures down.

And if this therapeutic mindset has reshaped how we parent and relate, how much more damaging is it when we instill it systematically into the minds of children?

Chapter Review: When Therapy Shapes Culture: Entitlement, Fragility, and Disconnection

✦ A Better Way Forward
Culture reflects the therapy it consumes. Entitlement, fragility, and self-focus have become normalized—but they are not virtues. To lead well in this culture, we must model strength, humility, and responsibility.

✦ Reflection & Response
- **Key Insight**: Culture has absorbed therapy's worst habits—entitlement, avoidance, fragility. We must ask: are we equipping people to grow, or enabling them to stay broken?
- **Challenge Question**: Have I absorbed cultural habits of entitlement or fragility?
- **Scripture Anchor**: 2 Timothy 3:1–5 – 'Lovers of self... having a form of godliness but denying its power.'

In Chapter 7: *SEL in Schools: A Systematic Reinforcement of Narcissism*, we'll explore how educational systems, through Social-Emotional Learning programs, are embedding emotional reasoning and entitlement into students—training the next generation to see feelings as facts, and the self as supreme.

Chapter 7:
SEL in Schools—A Systematic Reinforcement of Narcissism
When Emotional Safety Replaces Moral Development

Classrooms used to be places where children learned how to think, not what to feel.

They were trained to wrestle with truth, manage frustration, and build perseverance. Teachers reinforced discipline, guided students through conflict, and prepared them to engage the world with character and clarity. But somewhere along the way, the goal of education changed—from cultivating resilience to curating emotional comfort. And leading that shift is Social-Emotional Learning (SEL).

What began as a promising framework to help children grow in emotional intelligence has been hijacked by therapeutic ideology. SEL no longer primarily aims to build grit, empathy, or moral development—it reinforces the idea that feelings are the final authority and that emotional discomfort is to be avoided at all costs. Students are taught to center their feelings, demand emotional safety, and filter reality through their emotional responses. In short, SEL conditions children to become emotionally fragile and narcissistically self-focused.

This chapter will examine the evolution of SEL—from a character-based model of personal growth to a therapeutic system of emotional over-validation and ideological grooming. It will explore how this educational trend mirrors the very crisis seen in therapy: the replacement of truth, responsibility, and discipline with emotional entitlement and fragile identity.

1. How Social-Emotional Learning Promotes Self-Focus Over Resilience

The Original Intent of SEL

At its inception, SEL held noble promise. Developed to teach children how to understand emotions, regulate behavior, and relate well to others, it was built on sound psychological principles. It aimed to cultivate empathy, ethical decision-making, and a sense of social responsibility.

Programs like these once mirrored biblical wisdom—training children to become slow to anger, quick to listen, and humble in conflict. Emotional literacy was a tool, not an identity. SEL reinforced that self-control and social awareness were learned, not entitled.

The Turn Toward Over-Validation

But in recent decades, SEL has moved from building emotional regulation to fostering emotional centrality. Students are now taught that their feelings must be constantly validated and expressed—and never critically evaluated.

Rather than helping students work through disappointment or frustration, SEL-trained teachers are often coached to shield students from these experiences entirely. "Safe spaces," emotional check-ins, and "feeling circles" dominate the classroom, replacing character development with a therapeutic experience.

Feelings Over Facts

In the current SEL model, emotional expression is often elevated above objective truth. Students are taught that their internal experiences are the most important guide to reality. Instead of asking, "What is true?" they are taught to ask, "How do I feel?"

As a result, classrooms no longer reward perseverance, self-correction, or critical engagement—they reward emotional disclosure. A child who shares their feelings is praised more than a child who demonstrates resilience or rational thinking. Over time, this conditions young minds to believe their emotions define truth and that their discomfort signals injustice rather than a learning opportunity.

The Classroom Without Consequences

Ms. Robbins, a 5th-grade teacher, began every morning with a "feelings check-in." One day, when a student became upset after being corrected on a math problem, she encouraged the class to affirm him: "He's feeling sad, and that's okay."

The correction itself was never revisited. The wrong answer stood. The student's feelings were validated—but the learning moment was lost. In this SEL-driven environment, emotional comfort became more important than growth.

2. The Problem with Teaching Children That Emotions Dictate Reality

SEL and Emotional Reasoning

Emotional reasoning is one of the most harmful cognitive distortions, and yet, it is being normalized through SEL. When children are told to "trust their feelings," without learning how to test those feelings against truth, they are being set up for a life of emotional instability.

SEL's constant validation of emotions, without corresponding emphasis on truth, promotes narcissistic thinking: "If I feel it, it must be true." A child who feels slighted assumes injustice. A student who feels anxious believes they are in danger. No one teaches them how to question or reinterpret those feelings.

The Disrespected Student

Tanner, a 7th grader, received a B on his essay. He told his teacher it made him feel "disrespected." The teacher, trained in SEL methods, said, "I hear your feelings, and I'm sorry you feel that way." The grade stood, but the implication was clear: Tanner's feelings were as important as the facts.

No one asked if the grade was fair. No one reviewed the rubric. His emotional reaction was validated, and that was the end of it.

The Consequences of Emotion-First Education

When emotions override facts, children are not taught resilience—they are trained in grievance. They do not develop the ability to regulate their internal experiences; instead, they externalize blame and expect accommodation. Conflict resolution becomes impossible because objective standards are abandoned in favor of emotional consensus.

Children begin to believe that their discomfort is not something to grow through—but something others must remove. This creates a classroom culture of entitlement, where the most offended voice wins.

The Entitlement Mindset

When children are constantly affirmed without being challenged, they become emotionally entitled. They expect the world to validate their every feeling. Any form of correction is viewed as criticism, and any disagreement is perceived as personal harm.

Over time, this entitlement leads to an inability to adapt. Students grow into young adults who cannot handle correction, who view discomfort as oppression, and who believe their emotional needs should dictate institutional policies.

3. SEL as an Ideological Grooming Tool Rather Than a Resilience-Building Method

From Personal Development to Political Socialization

Perhaps the most troubling shift in SEL is its transition from teaching social skills to promoting ideological conformity. In many schools, SEL is no longer about learning how to manage emotions—it is about learning what to think and feel about social issues.

Modern SEL programs now include lessons on race, gender, sexuality, climate, and power dynamics—not as open discussions, but as emotionally charged affirmations of progressive viewpoints.

Undermining Independent Thinking

SEL does not encourage children to evaluate arguments or analyze evidence. Instead, it appeals to emotion. It asks children to "feel empathy" for certain causes and "stand up" for particular groups. While empathy itself is virtuous, using it as an emotional hook for ideological alignment is manipulative.

This creates students who do not question ideas but absorb them emotionally. They are not taught to ask, "Is this true?" but "How does this make me feel?" Those who challenge these narratives may be viewed as lacking compassion or being "unsafe."

The Biased Role-Play

At a middle school in Oregon, students participated in an SEL lesson about climate change. In their role-play, one student portrayed a climate "denier." The others were told to explain why their beliefs were "harmful" and how to "help them see the truth."

The lesson didn't promote debate—it punished dissent. The student playing the skeptic left the classroom in tears, feeling socially shamed. The message was clear: Feelings define morality, and disagreement is dangerous.

Psychological Coercion Through SEL

When SEL frames certain views as "compassionate" and others as "intolerant," it shifts from education to indoctrination. Children who disagree are labeled problematic. Teachers feel pressure to conform. Critical thinking is replaced by emotional allegiance.

This is not education—it is psychological grooming. And it exploits the very emotional vulnerability SEL was supposed to strengthen.

4. The Long-Term Consequences of Emotional Entitlement in Young Adults

Fragility in Adulthood

The students shaped by SEL do not leave their feelings at graduation. They carry them into college campuses, workplaces, marriages, and churches. And when life fails to validate them, they break.

Universities now build "safe spaces" and "bias response teams" to protect students from discomfort. Corporations implement sensitivity training not to teach resilience but to prevent offense. Emotional immaturity becomes the metric by which policies are designed.

The Rise of Therapy-Speak in Everyday Life

Terms like "toxic," "triggered," "gaslit," and "self-care" have become everyday tools—not for self-awareness, but for self-justification. These concepts, borrowed from therapy, are often weaponized to avoid accountability.

When a relationship gets hard, it's "toxic." When someone is corrected, they are "being gaslit." When a job is demanding, it's a "mental health crisis." The language of mental wellness is used to shield emotional fragility, not strengthen character.

The Quitting Employee

Jaden, a 25-year-old, quit his job after his manager asked him to stay late during a product launch. In his exit interview, Jaden said, "That was a boundary violation. I needed to prioritize self-care."

His coworkers were stunned. The request was reasonable. But Jaden had been shaped by a culture that taught him discomfort was abuse, and boundaries were excuses.

The Erosion of Grit and Critical Thinking

A culture that prizes feelings over facts cannot sustain growth. Without perseverance, people quit when things get hard. Without critical thinking, ideas go unchallenged. And without resilience, relationships fall apart.

The society shaped by SEL is not becoming emotionally intelligent—it is becoming emotionally indulgent. And the cost will be paid in every domain of life.

Action and Resolution: Reclaiming Emotional Maturity in Education

The path forward is clear. SEL must be reclaimed—not as a system for emotional affirmation, but as a tool for personal growth. Educators must:

- Teach that feelings are *real*, but not always *right*.
- Equip students to *regulate emotions*, not rule by them.
- Reinforce *accountability*, *critical thinking*, and *resilience*.

Emotional maturity is not built by centering feelings—it's built by guiding children through discomfort, helping them face challenges, and teaching them how to live by truth.

A Better Classroom

Mr. Hodge, a 6th-grade teacher, still uses SEL—but with wisdom. When students express frustration, he listens—but he doesn't stop there. "I hear that you're upset," he says. "Now let's talk about what's true. Let's solve the problem together."

His classroom isn't always "safe"—but it's always respectful, truthful, and formative. And his students grow—not just in feelings, but in strength.

Social-Emotional Learning, in its current form, has become a vehicle for reinforcing narcissism, emotional fragility, and ideological conformity. It prioritizes feelings over facts, affirmation over resilience, and identity over truth. And it is shaping a generation unprepared for the real world.

But the problem isn't only in schools. Therapy itself has adopted the same pattern.

Chapter Review: Emotionalism in Schools and the Crisis of SEL

✦ A Better Way Forward
In our effort to teach empathy, we've often abandoned resilience. SEL should equip students to face adversity—

not fear it. Emotionally grounded education requires truth, structure, and training in endurance.

✦ Reflection & Response

- **Key Insight**: SEL programs often teach children to over-identify with feelings, undermining resilience. True education teaches emotional regulation, not emotional indulgence.
- **Challenge Question**: What am I teaching children (or clients) about feelings and resilience?
- **Scripture Anchor**: Proverbs 22:6 – 'Train up a child in the way he should go; even when he is old he will not depart from it.'

In Chapter 8: *The Over-Emphasis on Feelings (Stage One: Exploration)*, we'll examine how therapy's first stage—emotional exploration—has become a permanent destination rather than a starting point. Clients are kept in cycles of emotional indulgence rather than guided toward growth, insight, or meaningful change.

Chapter 8:
The Over-Emphasis on Feelings

Emotional Exploration Without Insight or Action Is Not Therapy—It's Indulgence

Every healing journey must begin somewhere. In traditional therapy, the starting point is the heart—emotions, memories, wounds, and long-buried pain. This emotional exploration is necessary. It helps people name what hurts, face what's been buried, and begin to understand what lies beneath their patterns and choices.

But emotional exploration is not the destination.

In today's therapeutic culture, however, it often becomes exactly that. The first stage of therapy—intended to open the door to deeper insight and meaningful action—has become a self-contained experience of emotional affirmation. Clients are taught to stay there: to keep exploring, keep feeling, keep "processing." They cry, confess, unravel—and then do it again next week. And the week after that.

But they don't change.

This chapter will examine how therapy's overemphasis on emotional exploration has created a system that reinforces emotional dependency, personal stagnation, and fragile identity. Instead of guiding people toward transformation, many therapists now keep them comfortably stuck in a loop of self-expression. The result is not healing—but habitual self-focus masquerading as progress.

1. How Therapy Conditions Clients to Remain in Exploration Mode

Therapy has always involved emotional work. The first step is helping clients recognize and articulate what they feel. That's essential. But feelings must lead to insight. And insight must lead to action. The full process of healing requires all three.

Unfortunately, modern therapy rarely progresses beyond stage one.

The Three-Stage Model: Exploration → Insight → Action

Historically, counseling followed a time-tested structure:

1. **Exploration** – Identifying emotions and experiences.

2. **Insight** – Interpreting and understanding those emotions.

3. **Action** – Making behavioral and relational changes based on that insight.

Exploration is the gateway—not the goal.

But today's therapy often treats exploration as the entire process. Emotional expression is elevated to an almost sacred status. Clients are encouraged to "just sit with it," "feel what you feel," and "honor your inner experience"—again and again. While these phrases can be helpful in moderation, when they become the primary focus, they produce stasis instead of movement.

Therapy as Emotional Containment

Instead of helping clients grow, many therapists now function more like emotional containment chambers. They witness pain, reflect it back, and normalize it—but don't challenge it or guide it toward resolution.

Some therapists are afraid to move beyond this stage. Others are simply not trained to. The result? Clients spend years in therapy with little change—still battling the same emotions, still reliving the same traumas, still blaming the same people.

The Perpetual Explorer

Samantha, 36, had been in therapy for three years. Every week, she revisited the pain of her childhood—her parents' divorce, her mother's neglect, her father's silence. Her therapist was kind and affirming: "That must have been so painful. You're doing such important work just being here."

And Samantha felt seen. But her patterns weren't changing. She was still depressed, still unable to form healthy relationships, still stuck in the same job. She hadn't moved forward because her therapist hadn't invited her to. The emotional work had never transitioned into insight or change.

2. The Dopamine Reward System of Emotional Validation

There's a reason clients want to stay in stage one: it feels good.

The Psychology of Being Heard

When someone truly listens, validates, and reflects back our feelings, it produces an emotional high. Brain scans show that emotional connection releases dopamine and oxytocin—chemicals associated with reward, comfort, and trust. In other words, being validated feels good.

But if therapy becomes primarily about chasing that feeling, it turns into a form of emotional indulgence. Clients begin to associate healing not with change, but with being affirmed.

The Trap of Comfort

Because emotional validation feels safe and affirming, many clients resist moving toward harder work. Insight requires confronting unflattering truths. Action requires courage and discipline. Those don't release dopamine—they require effort.

Therapists, too, may resist moving beyond comfort. They fear pushing the client too hard. They fear being perceived as harsh. They fear making the client uncomfortable.

So they keep validating. And the cycle continues.

3. The Consequences of Perpetual Emotional Processing

Endless exploration without insight is not therapeutic—it's paralyzing.

Emotional Fragility

Without cognitive restructuring, emotions remain unchecked. The more they are affirmed without being examined, the more fragile they become. Clients become hypersensitive to discomfort. They interpret disagreement as harm, correction as rejection.

They are not being strengthened—they are being coddled.

Identity Confusion

When clients stay in the feelings stage, they often begin to identify with their emotions. "I feel broken" becomes "I am broken." Instead of learning to manage emotions, they absorb them into their identity.

This leads to deeper confusion. Clients no longer know who they are apart from their wounds. They cling to victim narratives, not because they want to—but because they've never been shown how to move past them.

The Identity of Pain

Jared, a 29-year-old artist, had survived childhood abuse. Therapy helped him name his trauma—but five years later, he was still telling the same story. When asked who he was, Jared would answer, "I'm a survivor." It was his core identity.

But Jared wasn't growing. He was defining himself by what had happened, not by who he was becoming. His therapist had never invited him to ask: Who are you beyond your pain?

Avoidance of Responsibility

Without a movement toward insight and action, therapy unintentionally teaches people to dwell in emotional self-justification. The focus remains on how others hurt them—not how they might grow, forgive, or change.

This reinforces blame-shifting and emotional dependence. Clients expect others to change so they can heal—rather than embracing the hard work of self-leadership.

4. How Therapy Has Replaced Challenge with Comfort

Therapists today are trained to be emotionally safe. That's good. But too often, safety is confused with softness. And the result is therapy that avoids the very tension required for transformation.

The Fear of Discomfort

Confrontation is now seen as unkind. Challenging a client's thinking is seen as invalidating. But growth doesn't happen without discomfort. Iron sharpens iron—not cotton.

Many therapists, shaped by client-centered and trauma-informed models, are hesitant to guide, correct, or teach. They mirror emotions, but don't interpret them. They listen—but never lead.

The Loss of Therapeutic Courage

In a cultural climate where emotional sensitivity is sacred, therapists risk being labeled as "judgmental" or "unsafe" if they challenge clients too directly. So they play it safe. They stay in the exploration zone, hoping the client will one day discover their own insight.

But many never do. Because most people need help getting there.

The Non-Directive Spiral

Carly, a therapist fresh out of graduate school, was taught to "trust the client's process." Her client, Mike, kept bringing up his infidelity—but never took responsibility. He blamed stress, his wife's emotional distance, and his childhood trauma.

Carly listened. She validated. But she never asked the hard questions: "Why did you choose this? What do you need to do now to make it right?" She didn't want to "impose judgment."

Mike kept exploring. But he never repented. Never changed. Never grew.

5. The Need to Restore the Full Counseling Process: Exploration, Insight, and Action

If therapy is to be effective, it must move.

- From feelings to meaning.
- From validation to truth.
- From pain to purpose.

Reintroducing Insight

Clients must learn to examine their beliefs, not just express their emotions. This requires metacognition: the ability to think about one's own thinking. It involves asking, "Is this emotion based in truth? What story am I telling myself? What lies have I believed?"

This is where transformation begins.

Calling Clients to Action

Insight alone isn't enough. Therapy must call people to act: to confront, to forgive, to take responsibility, to rebuild. Change comes not from what we feel or even what we understand—but from what we choose.

Action is not always comfortable—but it is always essential.

Therapists as Guides

The therapist's role is not just to reflect emotion—but to shepherd souls. To speak truth in love. To call forth courage. To walk with the client into discomfort—and beyond it.

This requires wisdom, humility, and strength. But it also requires conviction: therapy is not for comfort. It's for growth.

A Therapist Who Led

Andrew, a 40-year-old husband, came to therapy after his wife threatened divorce. He blamed her. He cried. He said he felt abandoned.

His therapist, after listening, said: "I believe your feelings are real. But what role did you play? Let's talk about that."

Andrew was shocked. But he kept coming back. And for the first time, he began to take ownership—not just of his emotions, but of his choices. Six months later, he and his wife were rebuilding—not because of emotional exploration, but because of truth and action.

Therapy that ends with exploration doesn't heal—it pacifies. It teaches people to feel deeply but think shallowly. To express emotion but avoid growth. To remain in process but never pursue change.

We must restore the full arc of healing: explore, understand, act. Emotional exploration is a beginning—but without insight and action, it becomes a form of self-indulgence dressed in clinical clothing.

Chapter Review: The Over-Emphasis on Feelings (Stage One: Exploration)

✦ A Better Way Forward

Staying in emotional exploration may feel safe, but it stalls growth. At some point, every client must be invited to look deeper. Reflection should open the door to insight—not become a cul-de-sac of indulgence.

✦ Reflection & Response

- **Key Insight**: Exploration is vital—but without direction, it can become circular. Counselors must listen deeply, but also help clients move beyond venting into reflection.
- **Challenge Question**: Do I tend to overstay in emotional exploration instead of moving forward?
- **Scripture Anchor**: Ecclesiastes 3:1 – 'To everything there is a season... a time to weep and a time to act.'

In Chapter 9: *The Missing Link—Lack of Intellectual Challenge* (Stage Two: Insight), we'll explore how modern therapy avoids the crucial step of cognitive deconstruction. We'll examine why therapists fear intellectual and moral challenge—and why true healing cannot happen without it.

Chapter 9: The Missing Link—Lack of Intellectual Challenge

When Therapy Avoids Truth, Growth Becomes Impossible

We live in a culture increasingly allergic to challenge.

Whether in parenting, education, or therapy, the impulse to shield people from discomfort has replaced the responsibility to guide them toward growth. Nowhere is this more evident than in the second stage of the therapeutic process—**insight**. Once a critical step in helping clients understand and change their lives, this stage has been largely abandoned in favor of comfort-driven emotional affirmation.

The result? Clients are left with unexamined assumptions, unchallenged cognitive distortions, and unresolved emotional dependencies. They leave therapy feeling "seen" but not strengthened, affirmed but not transformed.

Insight—the process of critical self-examination, truth-telling, and belief correction—has all but disappeared from modern counseling. In its place is a warm but directionless model of therapy that reinforces emotional reasoning, fosters entitlement, and stunts emotional growth.

This chapter will explore how modern therapy's refusal to engage in intellectual challenge has created a generation of clients who feel better but live worse. It will examine the essential role of cognitive confrontation, metacognition, and moral responsibility in true healing—and why therapy must return to the courageous work of helping people think clearly if it hopes to help them live wisely.

1. Why Professional Counseling Avoids Deep Cognitive Deconstruction

The Legacy of Cognitive Therapy—and Its Decline

In the late 20th century, **cognitive-behavioral therapy (CBT)** emerged as one of the most effective modalities in counseling. Its central insight was simple but profound: **how you think shapes how you feel and behave**. CBT therapists helped clients identify distorted thinking patterns, challenge false beliefs, and reconstruct more truthful ways of seeing themselves and the world.

But today, many therapists have abandoned this foundation.

In the name of empathy, therapists now avoid correcting faulty thoughts. In the name of trauma-sensitivity, they sidestep truth-telling. And in the name of inclusivity, they fear imposing any standard of right and wrong. What remains is therapy that affirms but never transforms.

The Client Who Couldn't Be Challenged

Lisa, a 28-year-old graphic designer, believed her coworkers were conspiring to undermine her. She had no evidence—just feelings. Her therapist, fearing to invalidate her experience, nodded empathetically, saying, "That must feel so isolating."

But Lisa's belief wasn't true—it was rooted in past relational wounds. What she needed was a therapist who could gently say, "Let's test that thought. What's the evidence? Could there be another explanation?"

Instead, her assumptions went unchallenged. And her paranoia deepened.

The Customer Service Mentality in Counseling

Part of the problem lies in how therapy is now framed. The therapeutic relationship has taken on a transactional feel: the client is the customer, and the therapist is the service provider. In this model, challenge feels like confrontation. And confrontation risks losing the client.

Many therapists now see their role not as guides, but as supportive bystanders—compassionate witnesses who echo the client's feelings without offering direction. But empathy without truth leads to stagnation, not freedom.

Insight Requires Disruption

True insight doesn't come wrapped in warmth. It comes through disruption.

It means confronting blind spots, exposing lies we've told ourselves, and acknowledging the uncomfortable parts of our story. But if therapy never enters that space—if it always stops at affirmation—it deprives people of the very process that makes healing possible.

2. The Danger of Allowing Beliefs to Go Unchallenged in Therapy

Therapy as a Mirror or a Window?

Therapists are trained to reflect the client's experience. That's important—but reflection isn't enough. Therapy must not only mirror emotions—it must become a *window to reality*.

When therapy avoids questioning the client's beliefs, it fails to offer that window. It locks the client inside their own perceptions.

The Unquestioned Narrative

Marcus, a 35-year-old father, came to therapy after his wife left him. He claimed she was "emotionally abusive" and "ungrateful." His therapist, wanting to support him, focused on validating his pain.

But Marcus never looked at his own anger, neglect, or selfishness. He left therapy feeling vindicated—but unchanged. And his next relationship ended the same way.

How Self-Delusion Is Reinforced

Clients often arrive in therapy with a story. Some stories are honest. Others are inflated, distorted, or self-serving. That's human nature. But therapy must be the place where those stories are examined—not enshrined.

When therapists fail to challenge a client's assumptions, they validate delusion. They reinforce false narratives. And the client leaves therapy with more self-righteousness, not more self-awareness.

Stagnation Through Unchecked Thinking

Cognitive distortions—like black-and-white thinking, catastrophizing, emotional reasoning, and personalization—are common traps. Left unchallenged, they become frameworks for interpreting life. Clients believe what they feel and never learn to ask, *Is this true?*

This leads to emotional stagnation. The client isn't growing—just rehearsing the same pain.

3. How Self-Reflection Has Been Replaced With Self-Indulgence

Self-reflection is critical to growth. But reflection without structure becomes indulgence.

The Hollowing of Self-Examination

In the past, reflection meant looking honestly at your life—acknowledging failures, identifying patterns, and owning your part. It required humility, courage, and a desire to grow.

But today, therapy often encourages **endless introspection without accountability**. Clients explore feelings without evaluating them. They examine experiences without questioning their interpretations. The result is more self-expression—but not more self-awareness.

The Never-Changing Client

Sasha, a 41-year-old executive, was in her seventh year of therapy. She could articulate every wound, explain every trigger, and describe every inner child. But she hadn't changed her behavior in years.

She had mistaken analysis for growth. And her therapist had never invited her to something deeper—*repentance, forgiveness, reconstruction.*

Cultural Narcissism and Therapy

Our culture celebrates radical self-acceptance. "You are enough," "Live your truth," and "Don't let anyone change you" are modern mantras. And therapy has absorbed these ideas.

Instead of saying, "You are capable of change," therapists now say, "You're perfect as you are."

This isn't therapy—it's flattery. True self-reflection involves seeing what's broken and wanting to become whole. It's the path of sanctification, not self-justification.

4. The Necessity of Metacognition in Emotional Healing

What Is Metacognition?

Metacognition is the ability to think about your own thinking. It's the moment when a client says, "Wait—why do I always assume the worst?" or "Why do I feel rejected every time someone sets a boundary?"

This level of reflection is the turning point in therapy. It's where emotions are subjected to scrutiny, and beliefs are tested for truth.

But most therapy today never gets there. Clients are trained to feel, not think. They are taught to accept, not evaluate.

The Thought That Changed Everything

Elijah, 38, came to therapy believing he was "unlovable." Every failed relationship, every moment of rejection confirmed it. Then one day, his therapist asked: "Who told you that? What if that belief is wrong?"

It was the first time Elijah questioned the script he'd lived with since childhood. It was the moment insight began. Not because he explored his feelings again—but because he challenged the thought behind them.

The Role of the Therapist in Guiding Metacognition

Therapists must reintroduce questions like:

- Is this belief true or just familiar?
- What's the evidence for this thought?
- Could there be another explanation?
- How might you be contributing to this problem?

These are not harsh questions—they are healing ones. They lead people out of emotional loops and into mental clarity.

Insight Requires Intellectual Humility

Growth begins when people are willing to say, "Maybe I'm wrong. Maybe I need to think differently." That's the power of metacognition—it creates a bridge between emotion and truth.

And it's a bridge therapy must rebuild.

Action and Resolution: Returning to Insight-Driven Therapy

It's time for therapy to recover its backbone—not by becoming harsh, but by becoming honest again.

- Validate emotions—yes, but test beliefs.
- Challenge assumptions.
- Invite reflection.

- Call for change.

Therapists must stop fearing discomfort and start trusting their clients' capacity for growth. True healing is found not in the endless echo chamber of feelings, but in the furnace of truth.

The Honest Breakthrough

Erica had always blamed her father for her insecurity. In therapy, she finally said, "Maybe I've stayed a victim because it's easier than changing."

Her therapist didn't rush to soothe her. She paused and said, "That's a powerful insight. What do you want to do with it?"

That moment changed everything. Not because Erica felt heard—but because she saw herself clearly. And then chose differently.

Therapy that avoids intellectual challenge creates fragile clients with well-articulated emotions but poorly examined beliefs. It validates feelings without clarifying truth. It keeps people in cycles of self-exploration, but never calls them to action.

But what happens when therapy not only avoids insight—but also refuses to guide clients toward meaningful, value-based action?

Chapter Review: The Missing Link—Lack of Intellectual Challenge (Stage Two: Insight)

✦ A Better Way Forward

Insight doesn't just explain what we feel—it reveals why we feel it. True insight demands courage, and counselors must gently guide clients toward truth, even when it disrupts old narratives.

✦ Reflection & Response

- **Key Insight**: Insight reveals the beliefs beneath emotion. Without it, clients may feel—but never understand. Counselors must help uncover the 'why' behind the pain.
- **Challenge Question**: Where am I resisting insight that might challenge my beliefs?
- **Scripture Anchor**: Romans 12:2 – 'Be transformed by the renewing of your mind.'

In Chapter 10: *The Fear of Guidance and Action* (Stage Three: Application), we will explore how therapy has become hesitant—even hostile—toward providing moral direction or behavioral change. We will examine why many therapists avoid suggesting next steps, and how this passivity leaves clients emotionally aware but directionless, permanently "in process" but never transformed.

Chapter 10:
The Fear of Guidance and Action

How Therapy's Reluctance to Lead Leaves Clients Stuck

There's a moment in every counseling process where the client is ready to move—but the therapist doesn't lead.

The feelings have been explored. The past has been unpacked. The insights have started to surface. But what comes next?

Action.

Or at least, it should. But in today's therapeutic landscape, that next step—application—is too often neglected. Therapy stalls out right where it should begin to gain momentum. Clients sit in a cycle of emotional awareness without being asked to apply what they've learned. And therapists, afraid of being too directive or moralistic, shy away from offering practical guidance.

This chapter addresses the third and final breakdown in modern therapy's process: the refusal to guide, direct, or challenge clients toward action. We'll examine why therapists avoid moral and behavioral leadership, the consequences of this avoidance, and how reclaiming the action phase is essential for lasting change.

1. Why Counselors Are Afraid to Impose Values and Moral Frameworks

Therapy once included guidance—rooted not in dogma, but in wisdom. Today, the pendulum has swung so far toward neutrality that many therapists fear offering any form of direction at all.

The Rise of Therapist Neutrality

Modern therapists are trained to provide a "safe space." That's not wrong—but the definition of "safe" has changed.

Safe no longer means *honest but respectful*. It now means *non-confrontational and morally agnostic*.

- Many therapists believe they must never impose a viewpoint, lest they overstep.
- Instead of offering wisdom, they pose open-ended questions: *"What do you think is best for you?"*
- The client becomes the only authority, and the therapist becomes a passive facilitator.

But this leaves clients without a compass. They came for help—and received only a mirror.

The Cultural Fear of Moral Language

Postmodern psychology promotes moral relativism. "There is no right or wrong," we are told, "only what's right for you." This thinking has deeply infected the therapeutic world.

- Therapists now avoid discussing values, character, or right vs. wrong.

- Ethical guidance is viewed as imposition, even when a client is engaging in destructive behavior.

- The fear of offending has overridden the call to lead.

But without moral clarity, therapy can't help people live well—it can only help them feel better.

The Consequences of the "Non-Directive" Model

When therapists refuse to guide, clients remain stuck in cycles of indecision, self-doubt, and emotional dependency.

- They are told to "trust themselves" without being taught how to evaluate their thinking.

- They are encouraged to "make space for all parts of themselves," including the ones that sabotage growth.

- They may spend years in therapy without ever being asked to take a step forward.

124 Dr Chuck Carrington

The Therapist Who Wouldn't Guide

Jen, a 30-year-old woman in a dysfunctional relationship, came to therapy hoping for clarity. She wanted to know: *Should I leave, or stay and try to change things?*

Her therapist said, "That's something only you can decide."

After six months of sessions, Jen felt more confused than ever. She needed moral clarity, practical wisdom, and guidance. But her therapist had been trained to provide neutrality—not direction. And Jen remained stuck.

2. The Role of Moral Courage in Effective Counseling

Therapists who refuse to lead may avoid conflict—but they also prevent growth. Effective therapy requires moral courage.

Counselors Must Lead—Not Just Listen

People come to therapy because something isn't working. They are confused, stuck, or in crisis. While empathy and insight are essential, leadership is non-negotiable.

- A good counselor says what needs to be said, not just what the client wants to hear.
- They offer direction—not control, but guidance based on truth.
- They help clients make wise decisions grounded in character, not just emotion.

Without this, therapy becomes emotional babysitting.

The Fear of Offending vs. the Necessity of Truth

Many therapists fear that offering guidance will offend or alienate their clients. But growth requires *discomfort*. Transformation demands truth-telling.

- A therapist's job is not to preserve comfort—it's to promote maturity.
- Clients need someone who will challenge their thinking, not just echo it.
- The best therapy moments are often the hardest ones—the ones where the truth breaks through.

The Truth-Telling Therapist

Carlos, a 45-year-old father of two, had been cheating on his wife for months. In therapy, he justified it by saying he "felt emotionally starved."

His therapist listened but then said firmly, "Your feelings may be real—but your actions are wrong. You are violating your commitments and your integrity."

Carlos was stunned. No one had said it so clearly. But that confrontation became the turning point in his healing.

Accountability Is Essential to Healing

Without accountability, therapy reinforces victimhood and blame. With it, clients begin to grow.

- Clients must be responsible for their thoughts, choices, and behaviors.

- Therapy must teach people to own their role in the pain they experience.

- Healing isn't just about understanding trauma—it's about changing patterns.

Therapists who lead with courage give clients the gift of clarity, structure, and the tools to act.

3. How Lack of Action Steps in Therapy Leads to Arrested Development

Without action, therapy becomes circular. Clients keep processing the same issues without progress.

Endless Exploration Without Change

Today's therapy culture often emphasizes emotional "processing" over behavioral change.

- Clients revisit the same wounds and feelings—week after week, year after year.

- Therapists encourage this, believing that deeper emotional awareness is the answer.

- But awareness without application is useless. Feelings need to lead somewhere.

The Forever Client

Marsha had been in therapy for nine years. She knew her attachment style, her triggers, her family-of-origin wounds. But she still struggled with anxiety, indecision, and relational chaos.

Her therapist had never given her goals, habits, or action steps. The work had been "open-ended." And so was her progress.

Psychological Consequences of Stagnation

When therapy avoids action:

- Clients become *dependent* on their therapist to manage their emotions.
- They avoid responsibility, preferring to "process" rather than change.
- They lose motivation, feeling more self-aware but no more empowered.

It's not uncommon for clients to spend years in therapy with no measurable growth. Why? Because they were never taught how to act.

When Therapy Becomes a Lifestyle

Therapy was never meant to be a way of life. It was meant to be a *tool*—a temporary structure that equips people to flourish outside the counseling room.

But today, many clients:

- Stay in therapy indefinitely, with no exit plan.
- Become emotionally enmeshed with their therapist.

- Never take what they've learned and apply it to the real world.

Healing doesn't happen in 50-minute sessions alone. It happens in real life—through habits, decisions, and discipline.

4. Practical Solutions for Restoring Action-Oriented Counseling

Therapy must return to its original purpose: to help people change.

Goal-Oriented Counseling

Every session should include movement.

- What's the issue we're working on?
- What progress was made since last time?
- What's the next step you will take this week?

Therapists must be willing to say, "Here's what you can do," not just, "How do you feel?"

Without goals, therapy becomes emotional meandering. With goals, it becomes transformative.

Reintroducing Cognitive-Behavioral Structure

CBT remains one of the most effective tools for lasting change. It's time to bring it back—with conviction.

- Challenge false beliefs.
- Restructure distorted thinking.

- Replace emotional assumptions with truth.

Therapists must stop coddling emotion and start confronting error. Not to be cruel—but to lead people into freedom.

From Insight to Action

Dylan had struggled with people-pleasing his whole life. His therapist listened, affirmed—and then gave him a challenge:

"Say no three times this week. Even if it's uncomfortable."

He did. And it changed him.

The insight was important. But the action sealed the growth.

Teaching Personal Responsibility

A healthy therapist equips clients to:

- Own their choices.
- Build disciplined habits.
- Make value-driven decisions.

This is the kind of therapy that builds men and women of *character*, not just emotional awareness. It calls clients to higher ground. And it works.

When therapy avoids action, it fails its purpose. Clients are left adrift—emotionally aware but directionless, dependent but not transformed.

Therapists must stop fearing guidance and start offering it. They must reintroduce clarity, structure, and courage into their work. Not every session needs to be a breakthrough—but every session must move the client closer to freedom.

Chapter Review: The Fear of Guidance and Action (Stage Three: Application)

✦ A Better Way Forward
Action is the fruit of healing. A counseling process that never arrives at change leaves the client dependent. Love challenges. Truth guides. And growth requires movement.

✦ Reflection & Response
- **Key Insight**: Action is where healing becomes visible. Too many counselors stop short, afraid to challenge. But truth without action is merely academic.
- **Challenge Question**: What is one area where I need to take bold action—not just process?
- **Scripture Anchor**: James 1:22 – 'Do not merely listen to the word... do what it says.'

In Chapter 11: *A Framework for Healthy Counseling*, we'll present a corrective model—a vision for what therapy could be again. One that blends emotional validation with intellectual challenge and personal responsibility. A framework for healing that produces resilience, clarity, and growth.

Chapter 11:
A Framework for Healthy Counseling
Healing That Strengthens, Not Softens

Therapy was never meant to be a sanctuary for self-indulgence.

It was designed to help individuals walk through pain, confusion, and trauma—toward healing, wholeness, and maturity. But as we've seen, modern therapy has veered off course. Rather than anchoring people in truth, it often indulges their emotions. Rather than challenging clients to live better, it comforts them while they remain stuck. Rather than cultivating transformation, it settles for validation.

This chapter presents a ***corrective model for healthy therapy***, a framework that reintroduces the essential components that counseling was built upon: emotional honesty, moral clarity, intellectual engagement, and actionable change. When these elements are restored to their proper place, therapy becomes not just a place of relief, but a path to resilience.

Balancing Emotional Validation with Intellectual Challenge

There is no question that emotions matter. The therapeutic process often begins with listening to pain, honoring grief, and making space for the unspoken wounds that clients carry. But feelings, while real, are not always right. They can be distorted by past trauma, shaped by faulty beliefs, or exaggerated by unresolved fear.

Healthy therapy teaches that emotions serve as *signals*—not sovereign truths. They are like dashboard lights, alerting us to something deeper under the surface. But just as a flashing check-engine light doesn't tell you exactly what's wrong, emotions must be interpreted. To take them as infallible leads to confusion and stagnation.

Take Jenna, for example—a 32-year-old teacher who told her therapist, "I feel like I'm not good enough." A lesser therapist might've stopped at validating her feeling. But her counselor asked instead, "Is that feeling grounded in truth—or shaped by a story someone else told you?" That one moment of redirection allowed Jenna to begin seeing herself not through the lens of emotion, but through the lens of truth.

Validation is important—but it must not be the goal. It is the gateway. When used properly, validation opens the door to deeper insight. But when it becomes the destination, it creates a cul-de-sac of emotional indulgence. Therapists must help clients understand their feelings, but then invite them to evaluate whether those feelings reflect reality or misinterpretation. Instead of asking only, "How do you feel?", a healthy counselor will eventually ask, "What is true here, and what needs to change?"

This is where intellectual challenge becomes essential. A therapist must gently and skillfully help the client examine their assumptions, question their interpretations, and test the story they've been telling themselves. Emotions need interpretation. Thoughts need reformation. A counseling process that honors both the emotional heart and the rational mind prepares people to navigate life with both compassion and clarity.

Integrating a Moral Framework into the Counseling Process

The soul craves more than insight—it craves integrity.

Modern therapy, under the influence of postmodernism, has increasingly avoided questions of morality. Many therapists fear that if they speak of right and wrong, they will be seen as judgmental or ideological. But therapy without moral grounding is like navigation without a compass. Clients need to know not only what they feel, but what is *right*. Healing requires more than permission— it requires *direction*.

Consider Daniel, a client in his late 30s who entered therapy convinced he needed to leave his wife. "I just don't feel in love anymore," he said. A therapist committed only to emotional validation might have nodded sympathetically and helped him process his feelings of disconnection. But his counselor instead asked, "What does love mean to you? Is it a feeling, or a commitment? And what does your vow mean now that it's being tested?"

That moral clarity changed the trajectory of Daniel's life. He stayed. He worked. He fought for his marriage. And he became a stronger man in the process.

Morality in therapy isn't about imposing dogma—it's about helping clients align their lives with truth, wisdom, and long-term flourishing. When therapy avoids those conversations, people are left without guardrails, chasing feelings that lead them nowhere.

Many of the most destructive behaviors that clients bring into therapy—affairs, addiction, avoidance, rage, deceit—are not only psychologically damaging, but morally wrong. Avoiding that truth under the guise of therapeutic neutrality is a disservice to the client's healing. People need to be asked hard questions: Is this choice consistent with your values? What will the consequences be, not just emotionally, but relationally, spiritually, ethically? Are you seeking comfort or character?

Virtues like honesty, humility, perseverance, forgiveness, and courage aren't optional—they're essential for emotional health. When these principles are reintroduced into the counseling room, therapy moves from being a place of comfort to a place of correction and construction.

Teaching Resilience Instead of Emotional Indulgence

If you spend too long comforting a person's pain without strengthening their spirit, you make them weak. Therapy must help clients become **resilient**, not just understood.

Healthy coping means learning to endure discomfort with grace, to redirect negative emotion into positive action, and to refuse the easy seduction of victimhood. Resilience is built not by revisiting pain forever, but by building the internal strength to rise above it.

Take Kenny, a 27-year-old man who struggled with confrontation. He had grown up in a home where conflict was explosive and painful. As a result, he avoided hard conversations at all costs. His therapist, instead of merely affirming his discomfort, gave him a challenge: speak the truth kindly, once this week, even if your voice shakes. Kenny did it. And in doing so, he began to rewrite his internal script. Not through analysis alone—but through action.

This is the heart of resilience: doing what's difficult because it's right. Mental toughness isn't about pretending nothing hurts—it's about deciding that pain won't have the last word. When therapy focuses only on feelings, it creates emotional fragility. But when it fosters courage, clarity, and conviction, it produces people who can withstand pressure without breaking.

Clients should learn that setbacks are not destiny. That anxiety doesn't have to define them. That guilt, once owned and addressed, can give way to freedom. And they should be reminded—often—that while their past may explain them, it does not excuse them.

Resilience is what allows people to leave the therapy office and walk into the world prepared to lead, to love, and to live with wisdom.

The Role of Community and Relationships in Healing

Therapy should never be the only place where people find support. Healing accelerates when clients are embedded in healthy relationships, accountable structures, and value-driven communities.

Yet modern therapy often reinforces an isolated, individualistic view of the self. Sessions become echo chambers, reinforcing the client's perspective while excluding the input of spouses, families, pastors, or mentors. While confidentiality is important, therapy becomes limited if it fails to re-integrate the client into a network of healthy relationships.

Ava, a 35-year-old woman, had been in therapy for years. She had processed her trauma, examined her family history, and explored every layer of her pain. But she still felt stuck. Her therapist finally said, "You know what I think you're missing? Community. You need people who will walk with you, not just listen to you." That was the turning point. Ava joined a Bible study at her church and began experiencing the kind of connection and accountability that no amount of introspection could provide.

Therapy must point people outward—toward their marriages, families, churches, and mentors. Relational maturity means learning to communicate honestly, to take responsibility in conflict, to prioritize long-term commitment over fleeting emotions.

True healing comes through a combination of introspection and interaction. The inner work must lead to outer change—change that is witnessed, supported, and reinforced by those who love us. Isolation breeds distortion. But in the context of faithful community, healing takes root.

Conclusion: Returning Therapy to Its Rightful Purpose

Therapy must be redeemed—not discarded.

It must return to its rightful place as a tool for clarity, courage, and character formation. That means validating emotion, but not idolizing it. Challenging thought, not merely echoing it. Calling for action, not just awareness. And grounding people in moral truth, not moral neutrality.

A truly healthy counseling model integrates emotional presence with intellectual honesty, moral direction, and actionable steps. It forms whole people—resilient, responsible, and rooted in wisdom.

If therapy is going to produce men and women of strength, it must stop accommodating weakness and start calling forth maturity.

But this vision cannot rest on therapists alone. The restoration of strong, healthy individuals also depends on families, educators, and faith communities taking up their roles once again.

Chapter Review: A Framework for Healthy Counseling

✦ A Better Way Forward

A healthy counseling model balances empathy and direction. The three-stage path—exploration, insight, action—provides the rhythm of real transformation. This is what clients truly need.

✦ Reflection & Response

- **Key Insight**: A healthy model of counseling balances empathy with challenge, emotion with reason, and comfort with direction. This is the path to real change.
- **Challenge Question**: How can I better integrate emotional support with truth and accountability?

- ****Scripture Anchor****: Micah 6:8 – 'Act justly, love mercy, and walk humbly with your God.'

In Chapter 12: *Correcting the Course—What Parents, Educators, and Churches Can Do,* we'll explore how these pillars of society can reverse the damage done by emotional overindulgence and help raise a generation rooted in strength, sacrifice, and biblical truth.

Chapter 12:
Correcting the Course—
What Parents, Educators, and Churches Can Do
Rebuilding Strength, One Soul at a Time

Culture is downstream from the home, the pulpit, and the classroom. If therapy has played a role in producing emotional fragility, victimhood, and narcissism, it is not the only culprit—and it cannot be the only solution.

Real transformation happens when the institutions that shape hearts and minds take responsibility for their role in cultural decline and commit to restoring what has been lost. Families must reclaim their authority and moral leadership. Churches must stop mimicking pop psychology and start preaching transformative truth. Educators must stop shielding students from discomfort and start cultivating wisdom, reason, and grit.

This chapter is intended to be a lament—it is a charge. The therapeutic tide that swept over the culture can be turned. But only if the people and institutions most invested in human development step forward with courage and conviction.

Restoring Authority and Responsibility in the Home

The family is the first classroom, the first church, and the first government in a child's life. Parents are the original counselors. They are not meant to simply observe or cheer from the sidelines—they are called to shape, train, and discipline their children.

Modern parenting, deeply influenced by therapeutic ideology, has abandoned this sacred duty in favor of permissiveness masked as empathy. Too many parents believe that acknowledging a child's feelings is the same as affirming them. In doing so, they teach children to obey their emotions rather than master them.

The result is a generation of emotionally fragile young adults who expect the world to accommodate their inner states rather than learning to regulate them. Children who are always rescued from discomfort never learn how to grow through it.

A healthy parent validates a child's emotions but does not surrender to them. When a child is angry, the parent listens—but also teaches how to express frustration respectfully. When a child is disappointed, the parent comforts—but does not lower expectations or erase consequences. Discipline, structure, and consistent consequences are not forms of cruelty—they are acts of love that form character.

I've seen families turn around dramatically by reintroducing simple principles: chores done whether the child feels like it or not, apologies given not because one "feels sorry," but because one did wrong, and expectations upheld even when emotions protest. These homes become havens of peace, not because conflict disappears, but because order is restored. Children in these environments learn early that emotions are real but not always reliable, and that long-term growth often demands short-term discomfort.

The antidote to victimhood is *responsibility*. When children are taught to take ownership of their actions—without excuses, without finger-pointing, without waiting for the world to change—they become capable adults. They learn that life is not fair, but that character still matters. They learn that effort often outpaces talent and that perseverance builds confidence far more than affirmation ever could.

Reclaiming Moral Clarity in the Church

The second pillar of cultural health is the church, which for centuries served as society's moral compass. But many pulpits have fallen silent—not in volume, but in conviction. Where once the church called people to repentance, it now calls them to self-acceptance. Where once it offered truth that pierced the soul, it now offers platitudes that soothe the ego.

This therapeutic gospel, baptized in sentimentalism, has stripped the church of its authority. It preaches comfort but not conviction, blessing without burden, healing without holiness. In its effort to stay relevant, the church has often abandoned the one thing it was uniquely called to proclaim: that transformation is not found in self-expression but in surrender to truth.

The church must return to its roots. It must once again be the place where sin is named, not rebranded as trauma. Where repentance is preached, not postponed in the name of emotional readiness. Where the cross is not a metaphor for self-care, but the cost of discipleship.

One of the greatest tragedies in Christian counseling today is the attempt to integrate faith and psychology by muting one and amplifying the other. But true biblical counseling does not merely accommodate psychological insight—it places it under the authority of Scripture. It teaches that while our emotions can reveal our pain, they must be submitted to God's truth. That while trauma may explain certain behaviors, it does not excuse sin. And that healing is not found merely in expressing our truth, but in aligning with God's.

Imagine a church where sermons regularly teach that perseverance through trial produces maturity, where believers are reminded that self-denial is not oppression but freedom, and where emotional sensitivity is not idolized but matured through discipline. Imagine church small groups where confession leads to accountability, not just validation. Where spiritual maturity is measured not by how "seen" people feel, but by how obedient they become.

It is in such churches that biblical counseling thrives. Here, the goal is not emotional affirmation but spiritual transformation. Such counseling challenges selfishness, corrects distorted thinking, and calls people to die to themselves in order to live for Christ. And it works—not by removing all pain, but by giving it purpose. Not by avoiding conflict, but by resolving it through grace and truth.

Restoring Intellectual Rigor and Moral Formation in Education

The classroom is now the frontline of cultural formation. And tragically, it has become a place where children are trained to feel—but not to think. Social-Emotional Learning, in its current form, teaches children that feelings are the lens through which all truth must be filtered. And that discomfort—whether emotional, intellectual, or ideological—is to be avoided, not overcome.

The effects are staggering. Students are taught to interpret disagreement as harm, challenge as trauma, and resilience as repression. In doing so, we are not educating—we are enabling fragility.

Education must be reclaimed as the training ground of the mind and the character. Schools must once again prize logic, reason, grammar, rhetoric, and moral courage. Instead of asking students how they feel about a subject, teachers must ask them what they think, what they can prove, and how they can refine their ideas. Emotions should not be dismissed, but neither should they be elevated above truth.

Critical thinking must be reintegrated into every subject. In history, students should be taught to weigh perspectives and evaluate consequences—not just to see events through modern ideological filters. In literature, they should be challenged to grapple with moral complexity—not just identify with characters' emotional experiences. In science and math, students should be expected to persevere, to struggle through difficulty, and to value objective truth over personal opinion.

Educators who hold the line on standards and discipline are not relics of a bygone era—they are the last line of defense against emotional chaos. A teacher who refuses to lower the bar teaches students that they are capable of rising to meet it. A principal who maintains order reinforces the connection between behavior and consequence. A school that rewards effort, humility, and respect prepares students not just to graduate—but to live well.

Of course, schools cannot do it alone. Parents must be vigilant in monitoring what their children are learning, both in curriculum and in the hidden lessons of ideology. They must engage in conversations at the dinner table, ask hard questions about classroom content, and reinforce truth when the world offers lies. If the school teaches victimhood, the home must teach responsibility. If the classroom breeds entitlement, the family must cultivate gratitude. Education is not neutral—and parents who are absent from it surrender their children to confusion.

Rebuilding a Culture of Strength, Truth, and Accountability

What's at stake here is nothing less than the emotional and moral future of our children—and by extension, our culture.

We cannot build a healthy society on the foundation of feelings alone. We cannot cultivate wisdom without truth, nor resilience without discipline. If we want to see fewer adults who fall apart under pressure, we must raise children who are trained to endure it.

The culture must be reoriented toward strength. In the home, that means discipline without cruelty, love without permissiveness, and expectations that stretch a child's character. In the church, that means doctrine over trend, repentance over affirmation, and a call to holiness that transcends self. In education, that means rigor over relaxation, facts over feelings, and instruction that cultivates both virtue and intellect.

Responsibility must be taught as a virtue again. Children must be trained to own their mistakes, make restitution, and move forward with humility and determination. Emotional health does not come from being coddled—it comes from being equipped.

Truth, finally, must be reclaimed as the cornerstone of formation. When truth is aligned with emotion, peace follows. But when feelings are enthroned above fact, chaos ensues. If our children do not learn to align their emotions with truth, they will spend their lives trying to align reality with their emotions—and they will fail.

The time for lamenting the culture is over. It is time to lead. Parents must parent. Pastors must shepherd. Teachers must instruct. And together, we must reject the soft lies of emotionalism in favor of the strong truths of moral formation.

Therapy alone cannot save a culture. But if families, churches, and schools rise to their calling, we can raise a generation that is stronger, wiser, and more grounded than the last.

But for this movement to take root, the counseling profession itself must change. It must stop perpetuating the very fragility that families, churches, and schools are working to correct.

Chapter Review: Correcting the Course—What Parents, Educators, and Churches Can Do

✦ A Better Way Forward

The restoration of culture begins in the home, the church, and the classroom. Therapy can support—but never replace—these pillars. We must raise truth-centered, resilient communities.

✦ Reflection & Response

- **Key Insight**: Change starts in the home, the church, and the classroom. Institutions must reclaim their roles in forming resilient, truth-centered individuals.
- **Challenge Question**: What steps can I take to help my family, church, or school restore strength and clarity?
- **Scripture Anchor**: Deuteronomy 6:6–7 – 'Impress these words on your children... when you sit, walk, lie down, and rise.'

In Chapter 13, *A Call to Reform Counseling,* we will examine how the field of counseling must be restructured—from its education programs to its core philosophy—to prioritize not emotional indulgence, but wisdom, strength, and responsibility.

Chapter 13:
A Call to Reform Counseling

Recovering the Purpose of Therapy in an Age of Emotional Collapse

Counseling is in crisis—not because it no longer exists, but because it no longer knows what it exists for.

Once a field rooted in helping people overcome hardship, confront falsehoods, and grow into maturity, professional counseling has gradually transformed into a refuge for emotional indulgence. Instead of guiding people toward clarity, discipline, and responsibility, therapy now too often invites them to dwell in perpetual self-analysis, validating their every emotion while avoiding any real confrontation with truth.

The result is a generation of clients who are more fragile, more dependent, and less capable of navigating the real world than ever before.

Like the previous chapter, this chapter is also not a lament—it is a mandate. Therapy must be reformed. It must be recalled to its original purpose: helping people live in alignment with truth, overcome emotional distortion, and grow in character and resilience. To accomplish this, reform must take place at every level—from the therapeutic encounter to the education of future counselors, from the ethical compass of professional organizations to the courage of individual practitioners.

Therapy must stop comforting people into weakness. It must begin, once again, to challenge them into strength.

Restoring Truth and Accountability in the Counseling Room

At the heart of therapeutic reform is a shift from emotional indulgence to intellectual and moral accountability. For too long, therapy has operated under the false assumption that feelings are sacred and unquestionable. Counselors, trained to remain neutral and nonjudgmental, often reinforce the client's emotional narrative without examining whether that narrative is true or helpful.

This must change.

The role of the therapist is not to serve as a comfort provider, endlessly listening and nodding without comment. The role of the therapist is to guide. Guidance implies direction, and direction implies standards. Clients do not benefit from endless validation—they benefit from clear, reality-based insight that moves them from emotion to truth, from confusion to clarity, from paralysis to purposeful action.

Consider a client who declares, "I feel worthless." A therapist's job is not to affirm that feeling. Nor is it to simply explore where the feeling comes from. The therapist must help the client examine whether the belief underlying that emotion is true. Is it based on fact or distortion? Is it rooted in reality or a wound? Is it worth keeping or worth challenging?

When therapy teaches people to evaluate their emotions, rather than obey them, it frees them from the tyranny of emotional reasoning. When therapy equips people to take ownership of their decisions and actions, rather than blame others or remain passive, it produces growth. And when therapy makes room for discomfort, correction, and accountability, it restores its original power to transform.

But this requires therapists who are not afraid to speak hard truths. It requires counselors who can ask the necessary questions: What role have you played in this? What actions have you taken to resolve it? What belief might you be holding that is keeping you stuck? These are not harsh questions. They are the questions of love—because love wants the best for the client, not just the comfort of the client.

Reforming the Education of Counselors

If professional counseling is to be reformed, it must begin at the root—within the institutions that train counselors in the first place. Much of what passes for counseling education today is little more than ideological conditioning. Future therapists are taught to prioritize empathy over truth, affirmation over action, and social advocacy over personal responsibility. They are warned not to impose their values, but they are simultaneously encouraged to promote therapeutic values that align with modern progressive ideals—identity affirmation, emotional expression, and resistance to discomfort.

This is not neutrality. It is indoctrination.

Counseling education must be returned to a foundation of evidence-based practice and intellectual rigor. Students must be trained in how to recognize and confront distorted thinking—not just to hold space for it. They must be equipped to lead clients through the process of cognitive restructuring—challenging assumptions, evaluating beliefs, and reshaping internal narratives according to reality, not ideology.

Courses in ethics must return to a serious exploration of moral philosophy. In fact, standalone ethics courses must be reintroduced to many masters programs altogether, having been dropped from the coursework in many counseling programs in recent years. Students must once again be asked to wrestle with questions like: What is the good life? What constitutes maturity? What makes a life worth living? And what responsibility do people bear for their own well-being?

This philosophical clarity is critical. Without it, therapy becomes directionless. Counselors cannot guide others toward wholeness if they have no conception of what wholeness is.

Moreover, counselor education must break its dependence on emotional neutrality as a virtue. Counselors must be taught how to challenge, not just empathize. They must learn that confrontation—when done with care and integrity—is not a violation of therapeutic ethics, but a vital component of therapeutic success.

To reform counseling education is to train a generation of therapists who are thinkers, not just feelers. Leaders, not just listeners. Healers, not just validators.

Recovering Courage in the Counseling Profession

Perhaps the most urgent need in counseling today is not for better technique, but for deeper courage.

Many counselors know that something is wrong. They know that therapy has become soft, indulgent, and ineffective. They know that affirming a client's feelings without accountability does not produce healing—it produces dependency. But they are afraid to say so. They are afraid of being labeled intolerant. They are afraid of losing credibility among peers. They are afraid of challenging cultural narratives that have been enshrined in therapeutic doctrine.

But therapy cannot be reformed by cowards. It must be reformed by counselors who are willing to stand apart from the crowd and say, "This is not working. We can do better."

Such counselors must reject the ideological conformity that has taken over professional organizations. They must question therapeutic models that promote entitlement, fragility, and victimhood. And they must have the resolve to challenge clients when necessary, knowing that growth often requires discomfort.

Counselors who reform their practice in this way will not be thanked immediately. But they will be effective. They will produce clients who leave therapy stronger than they arrived. Clients who are clearer in thought, firmer in purpose, and more grounded in truth.

These therapists will lead the field—not because they followed the crowd, but because they had the courage to lead.

Building Alternatives to the Mainstream Counseling Model

It is time to build new roads. The existing highways of the counseling profession are clogged with emotionalism, moral relativism, and ideological traffic. For those seeking a different destination—truth, maturity, and strength—new paths must be forged.

This means creating counseling models that are character-based rather than comfort-based. Counseling that focuses on developing virtues like humility, honesty, perseverance, and self-control. Therapy that invites people to grow—not just to express.

It also means creating counseling frameworks that are compatible with faith. Many people of faith feel alienated by secular therapy, which often undermines their beliefs or pathologizes their moral convictions. Faith-integrated therapy provides a better way. It sees the client not just as an emotional being, but as a moral and spiritual one. It aligns the therapeutic process with the pursuit of truth, integrity, and obedience to God's design.

Finally, it means promoting counseling models that emphasize resilience. These models teach clients how to face adversity, not flee it. How to reframe struggle as opportunity. How to push through hardship with discipline, not collapse under the weight of emotion.

New counseling organizations must emerge—ones that reject the emotion-first, ideology-driven norms of mainstream psychology. These organizations must train therapists in truth, ethics, responsibility, and resilience. They must develop licensure paths that do not require ideological conformity. And they must hold firm in the face of cultural pressure.

The good news is, such reform is already beginning. Faith-based training programs are growing. Networks of therapists committed to moral clarity are forming. The soil is fertile. The seeds are being planted.

But the harvest will only come if counselors, educators, clients, and communities commit to this path.

The Crisis and the Cure

The counseling crisis is not simply a professional failure—it is a cultural one. Therapy has mirrored a society that worships emotion, avoids responsibility, and distrusts authority. But just as therapy has contributed to the weakening of individuals, it can also be part of the solution.

To get there, we must reclaim therapy's original purpose: to help people become strong, not soft. To lead them out of confusion, not affirm them in it. To teach them to act, not just to feel. And to build within them the character, clarity, and courage they need to thrive.

This will require difficult conversations. It will require institutional reform. It will require moral courage.

But most of all, it will require a return to truth.

Therapy is not meant to make people feel better. It is meant to help them become better. When therapy aligns with truth, it restores. When it caters to feelings, it corrupts.

Let us choose restoration.

Final Word: The Path Forward

To the individual—stop making therapy a lifestyle. Use it as a launching point, not a resting place. Seek wisdom, not just relief. Act on what you know is right, even when you don't feel like it.

To the parent—raise your children to be emotionally strong, not emotionally entitled. Teach them that discomfort is not harm. Help them master their emotions, not be mastered by them.

To the church—do not cede your authority to therapists who preach a gospel of self-affirmation. Reclaim your role in forming lives. Offer truth that transforms, not therapy that indulges.

To the counselor—lead. Don't follow the drift of culture. Help your clients grow in discipline, not dependency. Be bold enough to say what needs to be said.

To our society—we will not survive emotional fragility. If we want a future of strong families, thriving marriages, and morally grounded citizens, we must return to the virtues that built them: truth, sacrifice, discipline, and faith.

This is the path out of the crisis. This is the call to reform. Let us answer it—with clarity, with courage, and with conviction.

Chapter Review: A Call to Reform Professional Counseling

✦ A Better Way Forward

Restoring therapy begins with restoring courage. Counselors must resist cultural conformity and re-anchor their work in truth. Healing happens where integrity and compassion meet.

✦ Reflection & Response
- **Key Insight**: Therapy must reform itself—professionals must have the courage to resist trends and return to truth, responsibility, and growth-centered models.
- **Challenge Question**: Am I willing to challenge popular trends in order to counsel with integrity?
- **Scripture Anchor**: Galatians 6:1 – 'Restore them gently... but watch yourselves.'

Chapter 14:
The Way Back
Restoring Counseling, Restoring the Soul

Healing is sacred. And so is truth. In a time when therapy has often lost its way—collapsing into ideological activism, emotional overindulgence, or fear-driven neutrality—the need for restoration has never been more urgent. Counseling was once a process that invited people to wrestle with truth, take ownership of their lives, and mature emotionally, morally, and spiritually. Today, it often stops at validation—affirming pain but avoiding responsibility.

This book has traced the trajectory of that decline: how early therapeutic models focused on growth, insight, and change, but were gradually replaced by feelings-first ideologies that confuse emotional safety with healing. We've seen how emotional reasoning, relativism, and activist narratives have weakened the therapeutic process—and in doing so, left individuals, families, and communities less resilient, less connected, and less whole.

But critique is not enough. We must rebuild.

To restore the soul of counseling, we must recover a vision of therapy that is both compassionate and courageous. Emotions matter—but they are not sovereign. Truth must be spoken—but in love. Clients must be heard—but also guided. Counselors must be present—but not passive. And for those who follow Christ, counseling must become not merely a profession, but a ministry—a sacred calling in service of healing, transformation, and truth.

Let us begin where all healing begins: with presence.

Presence is the sacred gift that creates space for transformation. It is more than physical proximity—it is emotional and spiritual availability. In Christ, we see the ultimate model of presence: the God who became flesh and dwelt among us. Jesus did not rescue from afar. He came near. He sat, touched, wept, and walked with the wounded. His presence was not indulgent—it was intentional. He didn't just validate feelings; He named truth, called people to repentance, and restored them to wholeness.

Presence, then, is the starting point—but it is not the destination. Presence must be paired with clarity. The counselor is not merely a mirror; he is also a guide. We are not neutral observers—we are redemptive companions. And companions need a map.

This is why we return to the three-stage model of counseling: *Exploration, Insight, and Action*. This rhythm, both ancient and enduring, reflects the path of genuine healing.

- In **Exploration**, the counselor is a *witness*, listening with empathy and spiritual discernment.

- In **Insight**, the counselor is a *teacher*, helping the client understand the beliefs, stories, and wounds beneath their pain.

- In **Action**, the counselor becomes a *coach*, challenging the client to take responsibility, make new choices, and walk in truth.

But in every stage, the counselor is ultimately a *shepherd*—present, wise, truthful, and redemptive. We do not coerce. We do not impose. But we do *invite* people to change.

Restoring the soul of counseling also requires restoring its courage.

In today's therapeutic climate, counselors are encouraged to affirm every identity, avoid moral language, and never challenge a client's worldview. But real healing requires disruption. It requires the courage to ask: *"I know this feels real to you—but is it true?"* It demands a willingness to confront destructive patterns, not with condemnation, but with conviction.

For Christian counselors, this means reclaiming our identity. We are not therapists who happen to be Christians. We are Christians who happen to be therapists. Our allegiance is not to the latest psychological trend, but to the timeless truth of the Gospel. We are called to embody Christ—not by preaching in every session, but by modeling His presence, His wisdom, and His courage.

We ask deeper questions. Not just "How does this make you feel?" but "What does this reveal about your heart, your beliefs, your values, your responsibilities?" We help clients see their pain not as their identity, but as a place where God can work. We do not reduce therapy to emotional comfort—we elevate it to spiritual formation.

We must also reject the modern habit of *infantilizing* clients. Therapy should not keep people tethered to their wounds. It should not reinforce helplessness or prolong emotional dependency. It should empower.

Clients must be reminded that their trauma does not define them. That they are not the sum of their feelings, their diagnosis, or their past. They are image-bearers of God, capable of change, worthy of love, and called to live in truth. Healing happens when people reclaim agency—when they take ownership of their thoughts, their choices, and their direction.

Counseling that empowers will equip clients with tools—cognitive tools, spiritual disciplines, relational strategies. It will call them to action. It will hold them accountable. And it will celebrate *growth*, not just emotional expression.

But therapy alone is not enough. We must restore the family, the church, and the community as partners in the healing process. Counseling should never replace these institutions—it should strengthen them.

Too often, clients are encouraged to create boundaries that sever them from community in the name of self-care. But healing happens in *relationship*, not isolation. Counselors should ask, "What role does your church play in your healing?" or "How can you rebuild trust with your spouse or family?" We must help people reconnect to the support systems God designed for their flourishing.

And finally, we must cast a vision of *wholeness*. Counseling is not just about symptom relief. It's about integration—where belief aligns with reality, emotions serve truth, and actions follow values.

Wholeness is not perfection. It is maturity. It is knowing how to feel *without being ruled* by feelings. To love *without fear*. To forgive. To suffer redemptively. To live with purpose.

So what now?

If you are a **counselor**, I urge you: reclaim your calling. Examine your framework. Are you challenging your clients to grow—or just affirming their pain? Are you leading them toward truth—or letting them drift? Your role is not to keep people comfortable. It is to help them become whole.

If you are a **client**, seek a counselor who will love you enough to speak the truth. Who will hold space for your sorrow, but also ask the hard questions. Who will equip you to act, not just feel. Your counselor cannot change your life. But *you can*, if you are willing to change your mind.

If you are a **pastor**, preach with courage. Refuse to reduce the Gospel to therapeutic slogans. Call people to die to self—and be raised to new life. Let your church be a place of truth, discipline, healing, and community.

If you are a **parent**, teach your children to face discomfort, to take responsibility, and to live by what is right—not just by what feels good. Build a home where truth is spoken and love is anchored in wisdom.

If you are an **educator**, stop teaching children that feelings are facts. Teach them how to reason. How to endure. How to discern. Expect more of them—and they will grow.

And if you are simply a **person**, trying to make sense of your story—know this: you are more than your feelings. You are not defined by your diagnosis, your past, or even your deepest wounds. You are a person made in the image of God—capable of growth, worthy of love, and called to live in truth.

The pain you carry does not disqualify you from healing. The confusion you feel does not exempt you from clarity. You may not know the way forward yet, but you are not stuck unless you choose to stay. Within you is the capacity to change, to think differently, to act bravely, to align your life with what is right rather than what is easy or comfortable.

There is more to your life than survival. There is purpose. There is dignity. There is wholeness. And that wholeness begins—not with perfect feelings, but with honest ones. Not with having all the answers, but with asking the right questions. Not with waiting for someone else to fix it, but by stepping into responsibility and choosing growth.

> Healing begins with **presence**.
> It continues with **clarity**.
> And it ends in **transformation**.

This is how we restore the soul of counseling. And this is how we reclaim our own.

Final Chapter: The Way Back – Restoring the Soul of Counseling

✦ A Better Way Forward
We are not defined by our pain. Truth, not emotion, must shape our lives. Restoring the soul of counseling means restoring the soul of the person—and calling them into transformation, not just comfort.

✦ Reflection & Response
- **Key Insight**: We end where we began: with presence, truth, and transformation. Counseling must guide people to wholeness, not deeper into self-focus.
- **Challenge Question**: Am I living from truth—or just feeling my way through life?

- **Scripture Anchor**: John 8:32 – 'Then you will know the truth, and the truth will set you free.'

Glossary of Terms

Action (Therapeutic Stage)

The third and final stage of therapy, where clients begin to make deliberate life changes based on their insight, developing new behaviors, habits, and relational patterns.

Affirmative Therapy

A counseling model that prioritizes validating a client's stated identity or beliefs without question or critical reflection. Often avoids exploration of underlying causes or alternative perspectives.

Client-Centered Therapy

A non-directive therapeutic approach developed by Carl Rogers that emphasizes empathy, active listening, and unconditional positive regard, allowing the client to direct the healing process.

Cognitive Distortion

Irrational thought patterns that negatively affect emotions and behavior. Examples include catastrophizing, emotional reasoning, mind reading, and all-or-nothing thinking.

Dopamine Loop / Reward Cycle

A brain-based pattern where emotionally charged behaviors trigger a chemical reward (e.g., dopamine), reinforcing the behavior even if it leads to unhealthy outcomes.

Emotional Fragility

A state in which individuals have a low tolerance for distress, disagreement, or correction—often resulting from over-validation and lack of resilience training.

Emotional Reasoning

The belief that one's emotions reflect truth: "If I feel it, it must be real." This distortion confuses emotional perception with objective fact.

Exploration (Therapeutic Stage)

The first stage of therapy, focused on naming, understanding, and expressing emotions in a safe environment without judgment or pressure.

Flooding (Emotional)

A psychological condition in which a person becomes overwhelmed by intense emotions, making it difficult to think clearly or respond constructively.

Ideological Activism in Therapy

When therapists promote specific social or political ideologies within therapy, often prioritizing cultural narratives over individual growth or biblical truth.

Insight (Therapeutic Stage)

The second stage of therapy where clients begin examining the underlying beliefs, assumptions, or narratives that drive their emotions and behavior.

Internalized Oppression

The process by which individuals absorb and adopt negative beliefs or stereotypes about their own identity, often shaped by societal messages.

Moral Relativism

The belief that moral truth is subjective and personal rather than universal. In therapy, this can lead to an avoidance of moral guidance or accountability.

Multicultural Eclecticism

A therapeutic approach that borrows from many cultural worldviews without a unified framework—often leading to moral neutrality or contradiction.

Narrative Therapy

A counseling method that helps individuals examine and reshape the personal stories and belief systems that define their identity and guide their decisions.

Postmodernism (in Counseling)

A worldview that denies absolute truth and favors subjective experience. In therapy, this often results in moral ambiguity and resistance to firm guidance.

Redemptive Counseling

A faith-based approach to therapy that integrates biblical truth, personal responsibility, and grace—aiming for both emotional and spiritual transformation.

Therapeutic Presence

The act of being fully present—emotionally, spiritually, and relationally—with a client. It reflects Christ's model of incarnational compassion and attentive care.

Therapy Addiction

A condition in which a person becomes dependent on the experience of emotional validation or therapist affirmation without progressing toward change or independence.

Validation

The act of recognizing and affirming a person's emotional experience. While essential, validation without truth or accountability can lead to emotional stagnation.

References

Beck (2011). Beck, J. S. (2011). Cognitive Behavior Therapy: Basics and Beyond. Guilford Press.

The Holy Bible, New International Version. Biblica, 2011.

Corey, G. (2017). Theory and Practice of Counseling and Psychotherapy (10th ed.). Cengage Learning.

Lembke, A. (2021). Dopamine Nation: Finding Balance in the Age of Indulgence. Dutton.

Maslow, A. H. (1943). A Theory of Human Motivation. Psychological Review, 50(4), 370–396.

McLeod (2013). An Introduction to Counselling. Open University Press.

Neenan, M., & Dryden, W. (2004). Cognitive Therapy: 100 Key Points and Techniques. Routledge.

Rogers, C.R. (1961). On Becoming a Person. Houghton Mifflin.

About the Author

Dr. Chuck Carrington, PhD, EdS, MA, is a Christian therapist, educator, author, and speaker with over 30 years of experience working with couples, families, and individuals—including trauma survivors, foster families and children, men recovering from pornography addiction, and the wives healing from betrayal trauma. He specializes in trauma, grief, and loss, with a focused practice in Christian counseling that emphasizes relational restoration in the wake of betrayal, infidelity, and emotional dysfunction.

Dr. Chuck's research explores innovative approaches to loss recovery, process addictions, betrayal trauma, post-traumatic embitterment, and the long-term impact of childhood family dysfunction. Blending biblical wisdom with evidence-based therapeutic models and a down-to-earth relational style, he brings compassion, clarity, and deep insight into how past wounds shape present relationships.

He is the founder of *Connect Christian Family Counseling*, where he walks alongside clients on their journey toward emotional and relational wholeness.

When he's not writing or counseling, Dr. Chuck enjoys reading, researching, leading workshops, and serving in local ministry projects. He also hosts free online support and discipleship groups. This book reflects his passion for bringing a practical, gospel-centered message to those navigating the complex challenges of modern life—helping them rediscover their identity and purpose in God's redemptive plan, and equipping them to grow in truth, strength, and grace.

If You Need Counseling or Help,

Dr Chuck offers Christian Faith-Based Counseling and Coaching in men's recovery from porn and cyber-addiction, Betrayal Trauma recovery for women, and restorative counseling to help heal and recover marriages after betrayal.

For a consultation via telehealth video, contact Dr Chuck to get more information on how to overcome the damage of betrayal and addiction. Use the website below to sign up for recovery and support groups, or to join Dr Chuck's online psychoeducational programs.

If you are looking for marriage enhancement counseling or coaching, Dr Chuck offers online webinars and forums to help Christian couples explore their marriage, and how it conforms to God's plan for marriage, to find forgiveness and healing, or to plan for an extraordinary marriage from the outset for engaged couples.

Believers should ask for the Faith-based community discount for the best possible pricing. Free groups include Healing Hearts for women damaged by betrayal, Overcomer's Group for men struggling with porn addiction and cyber addiction.

www.connectcounselor.com
Connect Christian Family Counseling
757 965-5450

How does that make you Feel 181

Other Titles by Dr Chuck Carrington
Available on Amazon

Feelings Don't Care About Your Facts: How emotional Reasoning Hijacks Logic
ISBN# 979-8-9892386-7-5

We've all been there—trapped in an argument where logic and reason are rendered useless, where emotions drive the conversation, and no amount of evidence seems to matter. Emotional reasoning can wreak havoc on relationships, leaving partners feeling unheard, frustrated, and stuck in cycles of conflict.

The Renewed Mind: Rebuilding Trust in Marriage by Overcoming Porn Addiction for Life
ISBN# 979-89892386-3-7

Porn addiction is established long before its strong hold is realized, usually at some point in an adult relationship. This book takes science, counseling, and Christian living into a long term curative process. Included is information and direction on how to understand the impact of a man's porn addiction on his wife or partner, how to increase victim empathy, and the step to restoring her safety so trust can rebuild.

The Renewed Mind companion workbook
ISBN# 979-8-9892386-2-0

The Renewed Mind Study Guide, designed to complement the groundbreaking book The Renewed Mind: Rebuilding Trust in Marriage by Overcoming Porn Addiction for Life.

The Loving Marriage: Jesus Reduce Me To Love. Lessons on living out 1 Corinthians in Marriage is ISBN# 979-8989238651

Scripture provides a simple yet profound road map to guide all marriages on their journey of love, and in this book, we will help you develop a personal expression of love within your marriage, rooted in timeless biblical teachings.

The Masculine Edge: A Field Guide to Strength and Character
ISBN 979-8989238644

Discover the Edge You Were Born to Carry. The Masculine Edge is a bold, honest, and deeply practical
anthology for men who want more than surface-level faith.

Check out Dr Chuck's *Seven Greatest Hits in Marriage Counseling*, a series of video supported coaching modules presenting his most effective tools to help couples exceed a typical marriage. At www.connectcounselor.com

**Connect Christian Family Counseling
757 965-5450**
DrChuck@connectcounselor.com

www.ingramcontent.com/pod-product-compliance
Lightning Source LLC
Chambersburg PA
CBHW050634160426